CHURCH
POTLUCKS

Table of Contents

2 ✳ Brunch for a Bunch

22 ✳ Vegetarian Bounty

40 ✳ Divine Meats

62 ✳ Super Salads

80 ✳ Seafood Feasts

Brunch for a Bunch

Go and enjoy choice food and sweet drinks, and send some to those who have nothing prepared. . . . The joy of the Lord is your strength.
Nehemiah 8:10 NIV

Aunt Marilyn's Cinnamon French Toast Casserole

1 large loaf French bread, cut into 1½-inch slices
3½ cups milk
9 eggs
1½ cups sugar, divided
1 tablespoon vanilla
½ teaspoon salt
6 to 8 medium baking apples, such as McIntosh or
    Cortland, peeled and sliced
1 teaspoon ground cinnamon
½ teaspoon ground nutmeg
Powdered sugar (optional)

1. Place bread slices in greased 13×9-inch glass baking dish or casserole.

2. Whisk milk, eggs, 1 cup sugar, vanilla and salt in large bowl until well blended. Pour half of mixture over bread. Layer apple slices over bread. Pour remaining half of egg mixture over apples.

3. Combine remaining ½ cup sugar, cinnamon and nutmeg in small bowl; sprinkle over casserole. Cover and refrigerate overnight.

4. Preheat oven to 350°F. Bake uncovered 1 hour or until eggs are set. Sprinkle with powdered sugar. *Makes 6 to 8 servings*

Breakfast Bake

    1 pound ground pork sausage
    1 teaspoon Italian seasoning
    ½ teaspoon salt
    6 eggs
    2 cups milk
    ½ cup CREAM OF WHEAT® Hot Cereal (Instant, 1-minute, 2½-minute or
        10-minute cook time), uncooked
    1 teaspoon TRAPPEY'S® Red Devil™ Cayenne Pepper Sauce
    4 cups cubed bread stuffing (potato bread recommended)
    2 cups Cheddar cheese, shredded

1. Brown sausage in skillet, pressing with fork or spatula to crumble as it cooks. Sprinkle on Italian seasoning and salt; set aside.

2. Combine eggs, milk, Cream of Wheat and pepper sauce in large mixing bowl; mix well. Add cooked sausage and bread stuffing; toss to combine. Pour mixture into 13×9-inch casserole pan; cover. Refrigerate at least 4 hours or overnight.

3. Preheat oven to 350°F. Remove cover and sprinkle cheese over casserole. Cover pan with aluminum foil; bake 30 minutes. Remove foil; bake 15 minutes longer. Serve warm. *Makes 8 servings*

Serving Suggestion: Serve this dish with fresh fruit.

Prep Time: 30 minutes
Start to Finish Time: 4 to 12 hours soaking, 45 minutes baking

Ham 'n' Apple Breakfast Casserole Slices

    1 package (15 ounces) refrigerated pie crusts (2 crusts)
    20 pieces (about 1 pound) thinly sliced ham, cut into bite-size pieces
    1 can (21 ounces) apple pie filling
    1 cup (4 ounces) shredded sharp Cheddar cheese
    ¼ cup plus 1 teaspoon sugar, divided
    ½ teaspoon ground cinnamon

1. Preheat oven to 425°F.

2. Place one crust in 9-inch pie pan, allowing edges to hang over sides. Arrange half of ham pieces in bottom. Spoon apple filling over ham. Arrange remaining ham on top of apples; cover with cheese.

continued on page 6

Ham 'n' Apple Breakfast Casserole Slices, continued

3. Mix ¼ cup sugar and cinnamon in small bowl; sprinkle evenly over cheese. Arrange second crust over filling and crimp edges together. Brush crust lightly with water and sprinkle with remaining 1 teaspoon sugar. Cut slits for steam to escape.

4. Bake 20 to 25 minutes or until crust is golden brown. Cool 15 minutes. Slice into wedges. *Makes 6 servings*

Note: This casserole can be assembled the night before, covered and refrigerated, then baked the next morning.

Pineapple Coffee Cake

  1 can (20 ounces) DOLE® Pineapple Chunks
  ½ cup packed brown sugar
  1 teaspoon ground cinnamon
  ½ cup chopped walnuts
  3 tablespoons butter or margarine, diced
  2 cups prepared baking mix
  2 tablespoons granulated sugar
  1 egg

• Drain pineapple, reserve ⅔ cup juice. Pat pineapple dry.

• Mix brown sugar, cinnamon, walnuts and butter in medium bowl; set aside.

• Beat reserved juice with baking mix, granulated sugar and egg in large bowl for 30 seconds. Spoon into 9-inch round baking pan sprayed with nonstick vegetable cooking spray. Top with half of walnut mixture, pineapple and remaining walnut mixture.

• Bake at 400°F., 20 to 25 minutes. Cool. *Makes 8 servings*

Prep Time: 20 minutes
Bake Time: 25 minutes

Biscuit and Sausage Bake

2 cups biscuit baking mix
½ cup milk
1 egg
1 teaspoon vanilla
1 cup fresh or frozen blueberries
6 fully-cooked breakfast sausage links, thawed if frozen
    Maple syrup, warmed

1. Preheat oven to 350°F. Spray 8-inch square baking pan with nonstick cooking spray.

2. Whisk baking mix, milk, egg and vanilla in medium bowl. Gently fold in blueberries. (Batter will be stiff.) Spread batter in prepared pan.

3. Cut each sausage link into small pieces; sprinkle over batter.

4. Bake 22 minutes or until lightly browned on top. Cut into squares; serve with maple syrup. *Makes 6 servings*

Prep Time: 10 minutes
Bake Time: 22 minutes

Hash Brown Casserole

6 eggs, well beaten
1 can (12 fluid ounces) NESTLÉ® CARNATION® Evaporated Milk
1 teaspoon salt
½ teaspoon ground black pepper
1 package (30 ounces) frozen shredded hash brown potatoes
2 cups (8 ounces) shredded Cheddar cheese
1 medium onion, chopped
1 small green bell pepper, chopped
1 cup diced ham (optional)

PREHEAT oven to 350°F. Grease 13×9-inch baking dish.

COMBINE eggs, evaporated milk, salt and black pepper in large bowl. Add potatoes, cheese, onion, bell pepper and ham, if desired; mix well. Pour mixture into prepared baking dish.

BAKE for 60 to 65 minutes or until set. *Makes 12 servings*

French Toast Strata

4 cups (4 ounces) day-old French or Italian bread, cut into large cubes
⅓ cup golden raisins
1 package (3 ounces) cream cheese, cut into small cubes
3 eggs
1½ cups milk
½ cup maple syrup
1 teaspoon vanilla
2 tablespoons sugar
1 teaspoon ground cinnamon
Additional maple syrup (optional)

1. Spray 11×7-inch baking dish with nonstick cooking spray. Place bread cubes in even layer in dish; sprinkle raisins and cream cheese evenly over bread.

2. Beat eggs in medium bowl with electric mixer at medium speed until blended. Add milk, ½ cup maple syrup and vanilla; mix well. Pour egg mixture evenly over bread mixture. Cover; refrigerate at least 4 hours or overnight.

3. Preheat oven to 350°F. Combine sugar and cinnamon in small bowl; sprinkle evenly over strata.

4. Bake, uncovered, 40 to 45 minutes or until puffed, golden brown and knife inserted into center comes out clean. Cut into squares. Serve with additional maple syrup.

Makes 6 servings

Golden raisins are more moist and plump than dark raisins. They are first treated with sulfur dioxide (SO_2) to prevent them from darkening, then they are dried by artificial heat, not the sun.

Brunch Eggs Olé

    8 eggs
    ½ cup all-purpose flour
    1 teaspoon baking powder
    ¾ teaspoon salt
    2 cups (8 ounces) shredded Monterey Jack cheese with jalapeño peppers
    1½ cups (12 ounces) small curd cottage cheese
    1 cup (4 ounces) shredded sharp Cheddar cheese
    1 jalapeño pepper,* seeded and chopped
    ½ teaspoon hot pepper sauce
       Fresh Salsa (recipe follows)

Jalapeño peppers can sting and irritate the skin, so wear rubber gloves when handling peppers and do not touch your eyes.

1. Preheat oven to 350°F. Grease 9-inch square baking pan.

2. Beat eggs in large bowl with electric mixer at high speed 4 to 5 minutes or until slightly thickened and lemon colored. Combine flour, baking powder and salt in small bowl. Stir flour mixture into eggs until blended.

3. Combine Monterey Jack cheese, cottage cheese, Cheddar cheese, jalapeño and hot pepper sauce in medium bowl; mix well. Fold into egg mixture until well blended. Pour into prepared pan.

4. Bake 45 to 50 minutes or until golden brown and firm in center. Meanwhile, prepare Fresh Salsa. Let stand 10 minutes before cutting into squares to serve. Serve with salsa.   *Makes 8 servings*

Fresh Salsa

    3 medium plum tomatoes, seeded and chopped
    2 tablespoons chopped onion
    1 small jalapeño pepper,* stemmed, seeded and minced
    1 tablespoon chopped fresh cilantro
    1 tablespoon lime juice
    ¼ teaspoon salt
    ⅛ teaspoon black pepper

Combine tomatoes, onion, jalapeño, cilantro, lime juice, salt and black pepper in small bowl. Refrigerate until ready to serve.   *Makes 1 cup*

Cranberry Coffee Cake

½ cup walnuts or pecans, coarsely chopped, toasted
¾ cup sugar, divided
 1 cup plus 1 tablespoon all-purpose flour, divided
½ cup (1 stick) plus 1 tablespoon butter, softened, divided
½ teaspoon ground cinnamon
½ teaspoon baking soda
½ teaspoon baking powder
½ teaspoon salt
 1 egg
 2 to 3 teaspoons grated orange peel
½ teaspoon vanilla
½ cup sour cream
⅔ cup dried cranberries

1. Preheat oven to 350°F. Grease and flour 8-inch square baking dish.

2. For topping, combine walnuts, ¼ cup sugar, 1 tablespoon flour, 1 tablespoon butter and cinnamon in small bowl; rub mixture with fingertips until well blended.

3. Sift remaining 1 cup flour, baking soda, baking powder and salt into medium bowl. Beat remaining ½ cup sugar and ½ cup butter in large bowl with electric mixer at medium-high speed 2 to 3 minutes or until light and fluffy. Add egg, orange peel and vanilla; mix well.

4. Alternately add flour mixture and sour cream to sugar mixture; beat at low speed until blended. (Do not overmix.) Fold in cranberries. Spread batter in prepared pan; sprinkle with topping.

5. Bake 25 to 30 minutes or until toothpick inserted into center comes out clean. Cool 5 minutes before cutting. *Makes 16 servings*

Chocolate Chunk Coffee Cake

1¾ cups all-purpose flour
1 teaspoon baking powder
1 teaspoon baking soda
½ teaspoon salt
¾ cup packed brown sugar
½ cup (1 stick) butter, softened
3 eggs
1 teaspoon vanilla
1 cup sour cream
1 package (about 11 ounces) semisweet chocolate chunks
1 cup chopped nuts

1. Preheat oven to 350°F. Grease 13×9-inch baking pan.

2. Combine flour, baking powder, baking soda and salt in medium bowl. Beat brown sugar and butter in large bowl with electric mixer at medium speed until creamy. Add eggs and vanilla; beat until well blended. Alternately add flour mixture and sour cream; beat until blended. Stir in chocolate chunks and nuts. Spread batter evenly in prepared pan.

3. Bake 25 to 35 minutes or until toothpick inserted into center comes out clean. Cool in pan on wire rack. *Makes about 18 servings*

Summer Sausage 'n' Egg Wedges

4 eggs, beaten
⅓ cup milk
¼ cup all-purpose flour
½ teaspoon baking powder
⅛ teaspoon garlic powder
2½ cups (10 ounces) shredded Cheddar or mozzarella cheese, divided
1½ cups diced HILLSHIRE FARM® Summer Sausage
1 cup cream-style cottage cheese with chives

Preheat oven to 375°F.

Combine eggs, milk, flour, baking powder and garlic powder in medium bowl; beat until combined. Stir in 2 cups Cheddar cheese, Summer Sausage and cottage cheese. Pour into greased 9-inch pie plate. Bake, uncovered, 25 to 30 minutes or until golden and knife inserted into center comes out clean. To serve, cut into 6 wedges. Sprinkle wedges with remaining ½ cup Cheddar cheese. *Makes 6 servings*

Chocolate Chunk Coffee Cake

Spinach Sensation

½ **pound bacon slices**
1 **cup (8 ounces) sour cream**
3 **eggs, separated**
2 **tablespoons all-purpose flour**
⅛ **teaspoon black pepper**
1 **package (10 ounces) frozen chopped spinach,**
    thawed and squeezed dry
½ **cup (2 ounces) shredded sharp Cheddar cheese**
½ **cup dry bread crumbs**
1 **tablespoon butter, melted**

1. Preheat oven to 350°F. Spray 2-quart round baking dish with nonstick cooking spray.

2. Place bacon in single layer in large skillet; cook over medium heat until crisp. Remove from skillet; drain on paper towels. Crumble and set aside.

3. Combine sour cream, egg yolks, flour and pepper in large bowl; set aside. Beat egg whites in medium bowl with electric mixer at high speed until stiff peaks form. Stir one fourth of egg whites into sour cream mixture; fold in remaining egg whites.

4. Arrange half of spinach in prepared dish. Top with half of sour cream mixture. Sprinkle ¼ cup cheese over sour cream mixture. Sprinkle bacon over cheese. Repeat layers, ending with remaining ¼ cup cheese.

5. Combine bread crumbs and butter in small bowl; sprinkle evenly over cheese. Bake, uncovered, 30 to 35 minutes or until egg mixture is set. Let stand 5 minutes before serving. Garnish as desired.

Makes 6 servings

Nutty Toffee Coffee Cake

1⅓ cups (8-ounce package) HEATH® BITS 'O BRICKLE™ Toffee Bits, divided
⅓ cup plus ¾ cup packed light brown sugar, divided
2¼ cups all-purpose flour, divided
9 tablespoons butter or margarine, softened and divided
¾ cup granulated sugar
2 teaspoons baking powder
½ teaspoon ground cinnamon
¼ teaspoon salt
1¼ cups milk
1 egg
1 teaspoon vanilla extract
¾ cup chopped nuts

1. Heat oven to 350°F. Grease and flour 13×9×2-inch baking pan. Stir together ½ cup toffee bits, ⅓ cup brown sugar, ¼ cup flour and 3 tablespoons butter. Stir until crumbly; set aside.

2. Combine remaining 2 cups flour, granulated sugar, remaining ¾ cup brown sugar, remaining 6 tablespoons butter, baking powder, cinnamon and salt in large mixer bowl; mix until well blended. Gradually add milk, egg and vanilla, beating until thoroughly blended. Stir in remaining toffee bits and nuts. Spread batter in prepared pan.

3. Sprinkle reserved crumb topping over batter. Bake 30 to 35 minutes or until wooden pick inserted in center comes out clean. Serve warm or cool.

Makes 12 to 16 servings

Bacon and Maple Grits Puff

8 slices bacon
2 cups milk
1¼ cups water
1 cup uncooked quick-cooking grits
½ teaspoon salt
½ cup pure maple syrup
4 eggs

1. Preheat oven to 350°F. Grease 1½-quart soufflé dish or round casserole.

2. Cook bacon in large skillet over medium-high heat about 7 minutes or until crisp. Drain bacon on paper towels; set aside. Reserve 2 tablespoons bacon drippings.

continued on page 20

Nutty Toffee Coffee Cake

Bacon and Maple Grits Puff, continued

3. Combine milk, water, grits and salt in medium saucepan. Bring to a boil over medium heat, stirring frequently. Reduce heat; simmer 2 to 3 minutes or until mixture thickens, stirring constantly. Remove from heat; stir in syrup and reserved 2 tablespoons bacon drippings.

4. Crumble bacon; reserve ¼ cup for garnish. Stir remaining crumbled bacon into grits mixture.

5. Beat eggs in medium bowl with electric mixer at high speed until thick and pale. Stir spoonful of grits mixture into eggs until well blended. Fold egg mixture into remaining grits mixture until blended; spoon into prepared casserole.

6. Bake 1 hour 20 minutes or until knife inserted into center comes out clean. Top with reserved ¼ cup bacon. Serve immediately.   *Makes 6 to 8 servings*

Note: Puff will fall slightly after being removed from the oven.

Delicious Ham & Cheese Puff Pie

    2 cups (about 1 pound) diced cooked ham
    1 package (10 ounces) frozen chopped spinach,
        thawed and squeezed dry
½ cup diced red bell pepper
    4 green onions, sliced
    3 eggs
¾ cup all-purpose flour
¾ cup (3 ounces) shredded Swiss cheese
¾ cup milk
    1 tablespoon prepared mustard
    1 teaspoon grated lemon peel
    1 teaspoon dried dill weed
½ teaspoon garlic salt
½ teaspoon black pepper
    Fresh dill sprigs and lemon slices (optional)

1. Preheat oven to 425°F. Grease round 2-quart casserole.

2. Combine ham, spinach, bell pepper and green onions in prepared casserole. Beat eggs in medium bowl. Stir in remaining ingredients except dill sprigs and lemon slices; pour over ham mixture.

3. Bake 30 to 35 minutes or until puffed and browned. Cut into wedges. Garnish with fresh dill and lemon slices.   *Makes 4 to 6 servings*

Vegetarian Bounty

When you have eaten and are satisfied, praise the Lord . . . for the good land he has given you.

Deuteronomy 8:10 NIV

Veggie-Stuffed Portobello Mushrooms

4 large portobello mushrooms, about 1¼ to 1½ pounds
   Nonstick cooking spray
2 teaspoons olive oil or butter
1 cup chopped green or red bell pepper
⅓ cup sliced shallots or chopped onion
2 cloves garlic, minced
1 cup chopped zucchini or summer squash
½ teaspoon salt
¼ teaspoon black pepper
1 cup panko bread crumbs* or toasted fresh bread crumbs
1 cup shredded sharp Cheddar or mozzarella cheese

*Panko bread crumbs are light, crispy, Japanese-style bread crumbs. They can be found in the Asian food aisle of most supermarkets.

1. Preheat broiler. Line baking sheet with foil. Gently remove mushroom stems; chop and set aside. Remove and discard brown gills from mushroom caps using spoon. Place mushroom caps top side up on prepared baking sheet. Coat lightly with cooking spray. Broil 4 to 5 inches from heat 5 minutes or until tender.

2. Meanwhile, heat oil in large nonstick skillet over medium-high heat. Add bell pepper, shallots and garlic; cook 5 minutes or until bell peppers begin to brown on edges, stirring occasionally. Stir in zucchini, reserved chopped mushroom stems, salt and black pepper; cook 3 to 4 minutes or until vegetables are tender, stirring frequently. Remove from heat; cool 5 minutes. Stir in bread crumbs and cheese.

3. Turn mushroom caps over. Mound vegetable mixture into caps. Return to broiler; cook 2 to 3 minutes or until golden brown and cheese is melted.   *Makes 4 servings*

Caramelized Onion Tart

2 tablespoons butter
4 cups sliced onions
½ teaspoon salt
½ teaspoon dried thyme
½ cup ORTEGA® Salsa
2 tablespoons ORTEGA® Diced Jalapeños
1 (9-inch) refrigerated unbaked pie crust
½ cup shredded Cheddar cheese

Preheat oven to 350°F. Melt butter in large saucepan over medium heat. Add onions, salt and thyme; stir to coat well. Cover; cook 5 minutes, stirring periodically to prevent onions from burning. Reduce heat; continue to cook and stir 15 minutes or until onions are golden brown and caramelized. Stir in salsa and jalapeños.

Place pie crust in 9-inch tart pan with removable bottom. Pierce dough several times with fork. Spread onion mixture evenly over crust.

Bake 20 minutes or until crust begins to brown on sides. Sprinkle cheese evenly over tart. Bake 5 minutes longer. Remove from oven; let stand 5 minutes. Carefully remove from tart pan. Serve warm or at room temperature. *Makes 6 to 8 servings*

Prep Time: 20 minutes
Start to Finish: 1 hour

For a great lunch or dinner item, use ORTEGA® Salsa Verde in the tart filling and serve it with a salad of mixed greens.

Quinoa-Stuffed Tomatoes

½ **cup quinoa**
3 **cups water**
½ **teaspoon salt, divided**
1 **tablespoon olive oil**
1 **medium red bell pepper, chopped**
⅓ **cup chopped green onion**
⅛ **teaspoon black pepper**
⅛ **teaspoon dried thyme**
1 **tablespoon butter**
8 **plum tomatoes,* halved lengthwise, seeded, hollowed out**

Or substitute 4 medium tomatoes.

1. Preheat oven to 325°F. Place quinoa in fine-mesh sieve. Rinse well under cold running water. Bring 3 cups water and ¼ teaspoon salt to a boil in small saucepan. Stir in quinoa. Cover; reduce heat to low. Simmer 12 to 14 minutes or until quinoa is tender and plump. Drain well; set aside.

2. Heat oil in large skillet over medium-high heat. Add bell pepper; cook and stir 7 to 10 minutes or until tender. Stir in quinoa, green onion, remaining ¼ teaspoon salt, black pepper and thyme. Add butter; stir until melted. Remove from heat.

3. Arrange tomato halves in baking dish. Spoon in quinoa mixture. Bake 15 to 20 minutes or until tomatoes are tender.   *Makes 8 servings*

Spicy Jac Mac & Cheese with Broccoli

2 **cups (8 ounces) dry elbow macaroni**
2 **cups chopped frozen or fresh broccoli**
2 **cups (8 ounces) shredded sharp Cheddar cheese**
2 **cups (8 ounces) shredded Pepper Jack cheese***
1 **can (12 fluid ounces) NESTLÉ® CARNATION® Evaporated Milk**
½ **cup grated Parmesan cheese, divided**
½ **teaspoon ground black pepper**
2 **tablespoons bread crumbs**

For a less spicy version, substitute 2 cups (8 ounces) shredded Monterey Jack cheese and a few dashes of hot pepper sauce (optional) for Pepper Jack cheese.

continued on page 28

Spicy Jac Mac & Cheese with Broccoli, continued

Preheat oven to 350°F. Lightly butter 2½-quart casserole dish.

Cook macaroni in large saucepan according to package directions, adding broccoli to boiling pasta water for last 3 minutes of cooking time; drain.

Combine cooked pasta, broccoli, Cheddar cheese, Pepper Jack cheese, evaporated milk, ¼ cup Parmesan cheese and black pepper in large bowl. Pour into prepared casserole dish. Combine remaining Parmesan cheese and bread crumbs; sprinkle over macaroni mixture. Cover tightly with aluminum foil.

Bake covered for 20 minutes. Remove foil; bake for additional 10 minutes or until lightly browned.

Makes 8 servings

Wild Rice, Mushroom and Cranberry Dressing

3 cups water
1 teaspoon salt, divided
1 cup wild rice
1 tablespoon olive oil
1 cup chopped mushrooms*
1 small red onion, finely chopped
1 celery rib, finely chopped
½ cup dried sweetened cranberries
½ cup chopped toasted pecans (optional)
⅛ teaspoon black pepper
½ teaspoon minced fresh sage *or* ⅛ teaspoon dried sage

*Shiitake mushrooms are preferred, but you may use your favorite mushroom variety.

1. Preheat oven to 325°F. Grease 2-quart casserole. Bring water and ½ teaspoon salt to a boil in medium saucepan. Stir in wild rice. Cover; reduce heat to low. Cook 45 minutes or until tender. Drain well.

2. Heat olive oil in large skillet over medium heat. Add mushrooms, onion and celery. Cook and stir 7 to 10 minutes or until tender. Stir in wild rice, cranberries, pecans, if desired, remaining ½ teaspoon salt, pepper and sage.

3. Spoon mixture into prepared casserole dish. Bake 20 minutes.

Makes 8 servings

Note: To toast pecans, spread in single layer in heavy-bottomed skillet. Cook over medium heat 1 to 2 minutes, stirring frequently, until nuts are lightly browned. Remove from skillet immediately. Cool before using.

Veggie and Cheese Manicotti

    1 jar (23 ounces) marinara sauce
    1 package (8 ounces) manicotti
    1 tablespoon olive or vegetable oil
    1 cup fresh or frozen chopped broccoli
    1 cup finely chopped mushrooms (optional)
  ½ cup shredded carrot
    1 teaspoon minced garlic
    1 container (15 ounces) ricotta cheese
1½ cups shredded mozzarella cheese, divided
    2 eggs, lightly beaten
    1 teaspoon Italian seasoning or oregano
    1 teaspoon salt

1. Preheat oven to 350°F. Spray 13×9-inch baking dish with cooking spray. Spread about ¾ cup marinara sauce into baking dish; set aside. Cook manicotti according to package directions. Drain and rinse pasta in cool water; set aside.

2. Heat oil in large skillet over medium heat. Add broccoli, mushrooms, if desired, carrot, garlic and 2 tablespoons water. Cook about 8 minutes, stirring frequently, until vegetables are crisp-tender and water has evaporated.

3. Place vegetables in large bowl. Stir in ricotta, 1 cup mozzarella, eggs, Italian seasoning and salt. Fill each manicotti with vegetable-cheese mixture. Arrange filled manicotti in prepared baking dish. Pour remaining sauce over top and sprinkle with remaining ½ cup mozzarella.

4. Bake 55 minutes or until edges are browned and bubbly.   *Makes 6 to 7 servings*

Prep Time: 25 minutes
Bake Time: 55 minutes

Parmesan Vegetable Bake

  ½ cup seasoned dry bread crumbs
  ½ cup grated Parmesan cheese
    2 tablespoons butter, cut into small pieces
    1 clove garlic, minced
    1 teaspoon dried oregano
  ¼ teaspoon black pepper
    1 large baking potato, cut into ¼-inch-thick slices
    1 medium zucchini, diagonally cut into ¼-inch-thick slices
    1 large tomato, cut into ¼-inch-thick slices

1. Preheat oven to 375°F. Spray shallow 1-quart casserole with nonstick cooking spray.

2. Combine bread crumbs, cheese, butter, garlic, oregano and pepper in small bowl; mix well. Arrange potato slices in prepared casserole, overlapping slightly. Sprinkle with one-third crumb mixture. Top with zucchini slices; sprinkle with one-third crumb mixture. Top with tomato slices. Sprinkle with remaining crumb mixture.

3. Cover; bake 40 minutes. Remove cover; bake additional 10 minutes or until vegetables are tender. *Makes 4 servings*

Baked Bow-Tie Pasta in Mushroom Cream Sauce

  1 teaspoon olive oil
  1 large onion, thinly sliced
  1 package (10 ounces) sliced mushrooms
⅛ teaspoon ground black pepper
  1 jar (1 pound) RAGÚ® Cheesy!® Light Parmesan Alfredo Sauce
  8 ounces bow tie pasta, cooked and drained
  1 tablespoon grated Parmesan cheese
  1 tablespoon plain dry bread crumbs (optional)

1. Preheat oven to 400°F. In 10-inch nonstick skillet, heat olive oil over medium heat and cook onion, mushrooms and pepper, stirring frequently, 10 minutes or until vegetables are golden. Stir in Ragú Cheesy! Sauce.

2. In 2-quart shallow baking dish, combine sauce mixture with hot pasta. Sprinkle with cheese combined with bread crumbs. Cover with aluminum foil and bake 20 minutes. Remove foil and bake an additional 5 minutes. *Makes 6 servings*

Prep Time: 10 minutes
Cook Time: 35 minutes

Black Bean Flautas with Charred Tomatillo Salsa

Salsa

- 1 pound tomatillos, unpeeled
- 1 small yellow onion, unpeeled
- 6 cloves garlic, unpeeled
- 1 jalapeño pepper*
  Juice of ½ lime
  Salt and black pepper

Flautas

- 1 can (15 ounces) black beans, undrained
- 1 cup vegetable broth
- 1 teaspoon salt, divided
- ½ teaspoon ground cumin
- ½ teaspoon chili powder
- 3 cloves garlic, peeled and minced
- ¼ cup chopped cilantro
  Juice of 1 lime
- 10 flour tortillas
- 2½ cups shredded Colby Jack cheese
- 1 cup seeded and chopped tomatoes (about 2 tomatoes)
- 1 cup thinly sliced green onions

Jalapeño peppers can sting and irritate the skin, so wear rubber gloves when handling peppers and do not touch your eyes.

1. For salsa, cook and stir tomatillos, onion, garlic and jalapeño in large, heavy, dry skillet over medium-high heat about 20 minutes or until soft and skins are blackened. Remove from skillet; allow to cool 5 minutes. Peel tomatillos, onion and garlic, and remove stem and seeds from jalapeño. Place in blender or food processor with lime juice. Blend until smooth. Season to taste with salt and pepper. Set aside.

2. For flautas, place beans and liquid, broth, ½ teaspoon salt, cumin, chili powder and garlic in medium saucepan. Bring to a boil over medium-high heat. Reduce heat; simmer 10 minutes or until beans are very soft. Drain, reserving liquid. Purée drained bean mixture with cilantro, remaining ½ teaspoon salt and lime juice in blender or food processor until smooth. (Add reserved liquid 1 teaspoon at a time if beans are dry.)

3. Preheat oven to 450°F. Spread bean purée evenly on each tortilla; sprinkle with cheese, tomatoes and green onions. Roll up very tightly and place seam-side down in 13×9-inch baking dish. Bake 10 to 15 minutes or until crisp and brown and cheese is melted. Serve with salsa. *Makes 5 servings and 2 cups salsa*

Black Bean Flautas with Charred Tomatillo Salsa

Baked Ravioli with Pumpkin Sauce

1 package (9 ounces) refrigerated cheese ravioli
1 tablespoon butter
1 shallot, finely chopped
1 cup solid-pack pumpkin
1 cup whipping cream
½ cup shredded Asiago cheese, divided
½ teaspoon salt
¼ teaspoon ground nutmeg
⅛ teaspoon black pepper
½ cup small croutons or coarse bread crumbs

1. Preheat oven to 350°F. Grease 2-quart baking dish. Cook ravioli according to package directions until tender; drain well.

2. Meanwhile, melt butter in medium saucepan. Add shallot; cook and stir over medium heat 3 minutes or until tender. Add pumpkin, cream, ¼ cup cheese, salt, nutmeg and pepper; cook and stir over low heat 2 minutes or until cheese melts. Gently stir in cooked ravioli.

3. Spoon ravioli and pumpkin sauce mixture into prepared baking dish. Combine remaining ¼ cup cheese and croutons; sprinkle over ravioli.

4. Bake 15 minutes or until sauce is heated through and topping is lightly browned.

Makes 4 servings

Italian Vegetable Strata

1 loaf Italian bread
1⅓ cups FRENCH'S® French Fried Onions, divided
1 cup (4 ounces) shredded mozzarella cheese, divided
1 small zucchini, thinly sliced
1 red bell pepper, sliced
5 eggs
2½ cups milk
⅓ cup (1½ ounces) grated Parmesan cheese
½ teaspoon dried oregano
½ teaspoon dried basil

1. Preheat oven to 350°F. Grease 3-quart shallow baking dish. Cut enough slices of bread, ½ inch thick, to arrange single layer in bottom of dish, overlapping slices if necessary. Layer ⅔ cup French Fried Onions, ⅔ cup mozzarella cheese, zucchini and bell pepper over bread.

continued on page 36

Baked Ravioli with Pumpkin Sauce

Italian Vegetable Strata, continued

2. Beat eggs, milk, Parmesan cheese, oregano, basil, ½ teaspoon salt and ¼ teaspoon black pepper in medium bowl. Pour over layers. Sprinkle with remaining ⅓ cup mozzarella cheese. Let stand 10 minutes.

3. Bake 45 minutes or until knife inserted in center comes out clean. Sprinkle with remaining ⅔ cup onions. Bake 5 minutes or until onions are golden. Cool on wire rack 10 minutes. Cut into squares to serve. *Makes 8 servings*

Prep Time: 10 minutes
Cook Time: 50 minutes

Rio Bravo Rice-Stuffed Poblanos

  6 **large poblano peppers**
    Cooking oil
  3 **cups cooked long grain rice**
 ⅔ **cup sour cream**
1½ **cups shredded smoked Gouda or Cheddar cheese, divided**
  1 **cup frozen corn kernels, thawed**
 ⅓ **cup chopped cilantro leaves plus additional for garnish**
    Salt and pepper to taste

Preheat oven to 400 degrees. Slit each pepper lengthwise so peppers can later be stuffed with rice filling. Carefully remove loose seeds and veins, keeping stem intact. Rub pepper generously with oil and place on baking sheet. Combine rice, sour cream, 1 cup cheese, corn and cilantro in a medium bowl. Season with salt and pepper. Divide mixture to stuff each pepper; sprinkle with remaining cheese. Bake in preheated oven 20 to 25 minutes, until peppers are crisp-tender and filling is heated through. Garnish with cilantro. *Makes 6 servings*

Favorite recipe from **USA Rice**

Rio Bravo Rice-Stuffed Poblanos

Southwestern Corn and Pasta Casserole

    2 tablespoons vegetable oil
    1 red bell pepper, chopped
    1 onion, chopped
    1 jalapeño pepper,* minced
    1 clove garlic, minced
    1 cup sliced mushrooms
    2 cups frozen corn
    ½ teaspoon salt
    ¼ teaspoon ground cumin
    ¼ teaspoon chili powder
    4 ounces whole-wheat elbow macaroni, cooked and drained
    1½ cups milk
    1 tablespoon unsalted butter
    1 tablespoon all-purpose flour
    1 cup shredded Monterey Jack cheese with chiles
    1 slice whole-wheat bread, cut or torn into ½-inch pieces

*Jalapeño peppers can sting and irritate the skin, so wear rubber gloves when handling peppers and do not touch your eyes.

1. Preheat oven to 350°F. Grease 3-quart glass baking dish.

2. Heat oil in large skillet over medium-high heat. Add bell pepper, onion, jalapeño and garlic; cook and stir 5 minutes. Add mushrooms; cook 5 minutes. Add corn, salt, cumin and chili powder. Reduce heat to low; simmer 5 minutes or until corn thaws. Stir in macaroni; set aside.

3. Heat milk in small saucepan until simmering. Melt butter in large saucepan. Stir in flour to make paste. Gradually stir in hot milk. Cook and stir over medium-low heat until slightly thickened. Gradually stir in cheese. Cook and stir over low heat until cheese melts. Stir macaroni mixture into cheese sauce; mix well.

4. Spoon into prepared baking dish. Sprinkle bread pieces over casserole. Bake 20 to 25 minutes or until bubbly. Remove from oven. Let stand 5 minutes before serving.

Makes 4 servings

Divine Meats

*Go, eat your food with gladness, and drink . . .
with a joyful heart.*   *Ecclesiastes 9:7 NIV*

It's a Keeper Casserole

  1 tablespoon vegetable oil
½ cup chopped onion
¼ cup chopped green bell pepper
  1 clove garlic, minced
  2 tablespoons all-purpose flour
  1 teaspoon sugar
½ teaspoon salt
½ teaspoon dried basil
½ teaspoon black pepper
  1 package (about 16 ounces) frozen meatballs, cooked
  1 can (about 14 ounces) whole tomatoes, cut up and drained
1½ cups cooked vegetables (any combination)
  1 teaspoon beef bouillon granules
  1 teaspoon Worcestershire sauce
  1 can refrigerated buttermilk biscuits

1. Preheat oven to 400°F. Heat oil in large saucepan. Cook and stir onion, bell pepper and garlic over medium heat until vegetables are tender.

2. Stir in flour, sugar, salt, basil and black pepper. Slowly blend in meatballs, tomatoes, vegetables, bouillon and Worcestershire sauce. Cook and stir until slightly thickened and bubbly; pour into 2-quart casserole.

3. Unroll biscuits; place on top of casserole. Bake uncovered 15 minutes or until biscuits are golden.   *Makes 4 servings*

Old-Fashioned Turkey Pot Pie

**1 package (18 ounces) JENNIE-O TURKEY STORE® SO EASY Turkey
Breast Chunks In Homestyle Gravy**
1½ cups frozen mixed vegetables, thawed
⅛ teaspoon black pepper
1 package (15 ounces) refrigerated pie crust, divided

Preheat oven to 350°F.

In large bowl, combine turkey breast chunks in gravy, vegetables and pepper.

Place one pie crust in bottom and up side of 9-inch pie plate. Spoon turkey and vegetable mixture over crust. Place top crust over filling. Fold edges of crust inward and flute as desired to seal.

Bake 50 to 55 minutes or until crust is golden brown.

Cut into wedges and serve. *Makes 4 servings*

Sausage Pizza Pie Casserole

8 ounces mild Italian sausage, casings removed
1 package (about 14 ounces) refrigerated pizza dough
½ cup tomato sauce
2 tablespoons chopped fresh basil *or* 2 teaspoons dried basil
½ teaspoon dried oregano
¼ teaspoon red pepper flakes
3 ounces whole mushrooms, quartered
½ cup thinly sliced red onion
½ cup thinly sliced green bell pepper
½ cup seeded diced tomato
½ cup sliced pitted black olives
8 slices smoked provolone cheese
2 tablespoons grated Parmesan and Romano blend cheese

1. Preheat oven to 350°F. Coat 13×9-inch baking dish with nonstick cooking spray.

2. Heat large skillet over medium-high heat. Add sausage; cook until browned, stirring frequently to break up meat. Drain fat.

3. Line prepared dish with pizza dough. Spoon sauce evenly over dough; sprinkle with basil, oregano and pepper flakes. Layer with sausage, mushrooms, onion, bell pepper, tomato, olives and provolone cheese. Roll down sides of crust to form rim. Bake 20 to 25 minutes or until bottom and sides of crust are golden brown. Sprinkle with cheese blend; let stand 5 minutes before serving. *Makes 4 to 6 servings*

Southwestern Enchiladas

1 can (10 ounces) enchilada sauce, divided
2 packages (about 6 ounces each) refrigerated fully-cooked steak strips*
4 (8-inch) flour tortillas
½ cup condensed nacho cheese soup, undiluted *or* ½ cup chile-flavored pasteurized process cheese spread
1½ cups (6 ounces) shredded Mexican cheese blend

Fully cooked steak strips can be found in the refrigerated prepared meats section of the supermarket.

1. Preheat oven to 350°F. Spread half of enchilada sauce in 9-inch square glass baking dish.

2. Place about half of one package steak down center of each tortilla. Top with 2 tablespoons cheese soup. Roll up tortillas; place seam side down in baking dish. Pour remaining enchilada sauce evenly over tortillas. Sprinkle with cheese. Bake 20 to 25 minutes or until heated through.   *Makes 4 servings*

Mexican Tossed Layer Casserole

1 cup uncooked rice
12 ounces ground beef
¾ cup mild picante sauce
1 teaspoon ground cumin
2 cups shredded sharp Cheddar cheese, divided
½ cup sour cream
⅓ cup finely chopped green onion
2 tablespoons chopped cilantro
½ teaspoon salt
⅛ teaspoon ground red pepper

1. Preheat oven to 350°F. Coat 11×7-inch baking dish with nonstick cooking spray.

2. Cook rice according to package directions. Meanwhile, heat skillet over medium-high heat. Add beef; cook until browned, stirring frequently to break up meat. Add picante sauce and cumin; stir well. Set aside.

3. Remove cooked rice from heat. Add 1 cup cheese, sour cream, green onion, cilantro, salt and red pepper. Toss gently and thoroughly to blend.

4. Spoon rice mixture into prepared baking dish. Spoon beef mixture over all. Cover with foil. Bake 20 minutes or until heated through. Sprinkle with remaining 1 cup cheese. Bake uncovered 3 minutes more or until cheese melts.   *Makes 4 servings*

Heartland Chicken Casserole

10 slices white bread, cubed
1½ cups cracker crumbs or dry bread crumbs, divided
  4 cups cubed cooked chicken
  3 cups chicken broth
  1 cup chopped onion
  1 cup chopped celery
  1 can (8 ounces) sliced mushrooms, drained
  1 jar (about 4 ounces) pimientos, diced
  3 eggs, lightly beaten
    Salt and black pepper
  1 tablespoon butter

1. Preheat oven to 350°F.

2. Combine bread cubes and 1 cup cracker crumbs in large bowl. Add chicken, broth, onion, celery, mushrooms, pimientos and eggs; mix well. Season with salt and pepper; spoon into 2½-quart casserole.

3. Melt butter in small saucepan. Add remaining ½ cup cracker crumbs; cook and stir until light brown. Sprinkle crumbs over casserole.

4. Bake 1 hour or until hot and bubbly. *Makes 6 servings*

Glass and ceramic bakeware absorb heat more slowly, making them great choices for casseroles and acidic foods.

Rainbow Casserole

5 potatoes, peeled and cut into thin slices
1 pound ground beef
1 onion, halved and thinly sliced
  Salt and black pepper
1 can (about 28 ounces) stewed tomatoes, drained, juice reserved
1 cup frozen peas

1. Preheat oven to 350°F. Spray 3-quart casserole with nonstick cooking spray.

2. Combine potatoes and enough salted water to cover in large saucepan. Bring to a boil. Boil, uncovered, 20 to 25 minutes or until potatoes are almost tender. Drain. Meanwhile, brown beef 6 to 8 minutes in large skillet over medium-high heat, stirring to break up meat. Drain fat.

3. Layer half of ground beef, half of potatoes, half of onion, salt, pepper, half of tomatoes and half of peas. Repeat layers. Add reserved tomato juice.

4. Bake, covered, about 40 minutes or until most liquid is absorbed.

Makes 4 to 6 servings

Turkey and Mushroom Wild Rice Casserole

2 tablespoons butter
1 cup sliced fresh mushrooms *or* 1 can (4 ounces) sliced mushrooms
1 small onion, chopped
1 stalk celery, chopped
2 cups diced cooked turkey breast
1 can (about 10¾ ounces) condensed cream of mushroom soup, undiluted
1 pouch (about 9 ounces) ready-to-serve wild rice
1 cup milk
2 tablespoons minced fresh chives
¼ teaspoon black pepper
½ cup chopped pecans

1. Preheat oven to 350°F. Melt butter in large nonstick skillet over medium heat. Add mushrooms, onion and celery; cook 5 minutes or until onion is translucent. Stir in turkey, soup, rice, milk, chives and pepper; mix well.

2. Spoon mixture into 2-quart baking dish. Sprinkle with pecans. Bake 15 to 18 minutes or until hot and bubbly.

Makes 4 servings

Rainbow Casserole

Cousin Arlene's Spaghetti Lasagna

8 ounces uncooked spaghetti or other thin pasta
1 tablespoon butter
1 clove garlic, finely chopped
2 pounds ground beef
1 teaspoon sugar
   Salt and black pepper
2 cans (8 ounces each) tomato sauce
1 can (6 ounces) tomato paste
1 cup (8 ounces) sour cream
1 package (3 ounces) cream cheese, softened
6 green onions, chopped
¼ cup grated Parmesan cheese

1. Preheat oven to 350°F. Cook spaghetti according to package directions; drain.

2. Meanwhile, melt butter in large skillet over medium heat. Add garlic; cook and stir 1 minute. Add ground beef, sugar, salt and pepper. Cook and stir until browned; drain fat. Add tomato sauce and tomato paste; simmer 20 minutes, stirring occasionally.

3. Meanwhile, beat sour cream and cream cheese in medium bowl until smooth. Stir in green onions.

4. Spread ½ cup meat sauce in 2-quart casserole to prevent noodles from sticking. Layer half of spaghetti, half of sour cream mixture and half of meat mixture. Repeat layers. Sprinkle with Parmesan cheese. Bake 35 minutes or until heated through.

Makes 6 servings

This casserole can be frozen. Thaw it in the refrigerator overnight, then let it come to room temperature before baking.

Old-Fashioned Cabbage Rolls

8 ounces ground beef
8 ounces ground veal
8 ounces ground pork
1 small onion, chopped
2 eggs, lightly beaten
½ cup dry bread crumbs
1 teaspoon salt
1 teaspoon molasses
¼ teaspoon ground ginger
¼ teaspoon ground nutmeg
¼ teaspoon ground allspice
1 large head cabbage, separated into leaves
3 cups boiling water
¼ cup (½ stick) butter
½ cup milk, plus additional if necessary
1 tablespoon cornstarch

1. Combine beef, veal, pork and onion in large bowl. Combine eggs, bread crumbs, salt, molasses, ginger, nutmeg and allspice in medium bowl; mix well. Add to meat mixture; stir until well blended.

2. Drop cabbage leaves into boiling water 3 minutes. Remove with slotted spoon; reserve ½ cup of boiling liquid.

3. Preheat oven to 375°F. Place about 2 tablespoons meat mixture about 1 inch from stem end of each cabbage leaf. Fold sides in and roll up, fastening with toothpicks, if necessary.

4. Heat butter in large skillet over medium-high heat. Add cabbage rolls, 3 or 4 at a time; brown on all sides. Arrange rolls, seam side down, in single layer in casserole. Combine reserved boiling liquid with butter remaining in skillet; pour over cabbage rolls.

5. Bake 1 hour. Carefully drain accumulated pan juices into measuring cup. Return cabbage rolls to oven.

6. Add enough milk to pan juices to equal 1 cup. Pour milk mixture into small saucepan. Stir in cornstarch; bring to a boil, stirring constantly until sauce is thickened. Pour over cabbage rolls. Bake 15 minutes more or until sauce is browned and cabbage is tender.

Makes 8 servings

Spicy Chicken Casserole with Corn Bread

2 tablespoons olive oil
4 boneless skinless chicken breasts, cut into bite-size pieces
1 package (about 1 ounce) taco seasoning mix
1 can (about 15 ounces) black beans, rinsed and drained
1 can (about 14 ounces) diced tomatoes, drained
1 can (about 10 ounces) Mexican-style corn, drained
1 can (about 4 ounces) diced mild green chiles, drained
½ cup mild salsa
1 box (about 8 ounces) corn bread mix, plus ingredients to prepare mix
½ cup (2 ounces) shredded Cheddar cheese
¼ cup chopped red bell pepper

1. Preheat oven to 350°F. Spray 2-quart casserole with nonstick cooking spray. Heat oil in large skillet over medium heat. Cook chicken until no longer pink in center.

2. Sprinkle taco seasoning over chicken. Add black beans, tomatoes, corn, chiles and salsa; stir until well blended. Transfer to prepared dish.

3. Prepare corn bread mix according to package directions, adding cheese and bell pepper. Spread batter over chicken mixture.

4. Bake 30 minutes or until corn bread is golden brown. *Makes 4 to 6 servings*

Tortilla Beef Casserole

1 package (about 17 ounces) refrigerated fully cooked beef pot roast in gravy*
6 (6-inch) corn tortillas, cut into 1-inch pieces
1 jar (16 ounces) salsa
1½ cups corn kernels
1 cup canned black or pinto beans, rinsed and drained
1 cup (4 ounces) shredded Mexican cheese blend

Fully cooked beef pot roast can be found in the refrigerated prepared meats section of the supermarket.

1. Preheat oven to 350°F. Lightly spray 11×7-inch casserole or 2-quart casserole with nonstick cooking spray.

2. Drain and discard gravy from pot roast; cut or shred beef into bite-size pieces.

3. Combine beef, tortillas, salsa, corn and beans in large bowl; mix well. Transfer to prepared casserole. Bake 20 minutes or until heated through. Sprinkle with cheese; bake 5 minutes or until cheese is melted. *Makes 4 servings*

Spicy Chicken Casserole with Corn Bread

Layered Pasta Casserole

8 ounces uncooked penne pasta
8 ounces mild Italian sausage, casings removed
8 ounces ground beef
1 jar (about 26 ounces) pasta sauce
2 cups (8 ounces) shredded mozzarella cheese, divided
1 package (10 ounces) frozen chopped spinach, thawed and squeezed dry
1 cup whole milk ricotta cheese
½ cup grated Parmesan cheese
1 egg
2 tablespoons chopped fresh basil *or* 2 teaspoons dried basil
1 teaspoon salt

1. Preheat oven to 350°F. Spray 13×9-inch baking dish with nonstick cooking spray. Cook pasta according to package directions; drain. Transfer to prepared dish.

2. Meanwhile, cook sausage and ground beef in large skillet over medium-high heat until browned, stirring to break up meat. Drain fat. Add pasta sauce; mix well. Add half of meat sauce to pasta; toss to coat.

3. Combine 1 cup mozzarella, spinach, ricotta, Parmesan, egg, basil and salt in medium bowl. Spoon small mounds of spinach mixture over pasta mixture; spread evenly with back of spoon. Top with remaining meat sauce; sprinkle with remaining 1 cup mozzarella. Bake, uncovered, 30 minutes.   *Makes 6 to 8 servings*

Layered Pasta Casserole

Creamy Chile and Chicken Casserole

  3 tablespoons butter, divided
  2 jalapeño peppers,* seeded and finely chopped
  2 tablespoons all-purpose flour
½ cup whipping cream
  1 cup chicken broth
  1 cup (4 ounces) shredded sharp Cheddar cheese
  1 cup (4 ounces) shredded Asiago cheese
  1 cup sliced mushrooms
  1 yellow squash, chopped
  1 red bell pepper, chopped
  1 stalk celery, chopped
 12 ounces diced cooked chicken breast
¼ cup chopped green onions
¼ teaspoon salt
¼ teaspoon black pepper
½ cup sliced almonds

*Jalapeño peppers can sting and irritate the skin, so wear rubber gloves when handling peppers and do not touch your eyes.

1. Preheat oven to 350°F. Melt 2 tablespoons butter in medium saucepan. Add jalapeños; cook and stir 1 minute over high heat. Add flour; stir to make paste. Add cream; stir until thickened. Add broth; stir until smooth. Gradually add cheeses; stir until melted.

2. Melt remaining 1 tablespoon butter in large skillet. Add mushrooms, squash, bell pepper and celery. Cook and stir over high heat 3 to 5 minutes or until vegetables are tender. Remove from heat. Stir in chicken, green onions, salt and black pepper. Stir in cheese sauce.

3. Spoon mixture into shallow 2-quart casserole dish. Sprinkle with almonds. Bake 10 minutes or until casserole is hot and bubbly. *Makes 6 servings*

Pork and Corn Bread Stuffing Casserole

½ **teaspoon paprika**
¼ **teaspoon salt**
¼ **teaspoon garlic powder**
¼ **teaspoon black pepper**
4 **bone-in pork chops (about 1¾ pounds)**
2 **tablespoons butter**
1½ **cups chopped onions**
¾ **cup thinly sliced celery**
¾ **cup matchstick carrots***
¼ **cup chopped fresh parsley**
1 **can (about 14 ounces) chicken broth**
4 **cups corn bread stuffing**

Matchstick carrots are sometimes called shredded carrots, and are sold with other prepared vegetables in the supermarket produce section.

1. Preheat oven to 350°F. Lightly coat 13×9-inch baking dish with nonstick cooking spray.

2. Combine paprika, salt, garlic powder and pepper in small bowl. Season both sides of pork chops with paprika mixture.

3. Melt butter in large skillet over medium-high heat. Add pork chops; cook 2 minutes or just until browned. Turn; cook 1 minute. Transfer to plate; set aside.

4. Add onions, celery, carrots and parsley to skillet. Cook and stir 4 minutes or until onions are translucent. Add broth; bring to a boil over high heat. Remove from heat; add stuffing and fluff with fork.

5. Transfer mixture to prepared baking dish. Place pork chops on top. Cover; bake 25 minutes or until pork is no longer pink in center. *Makes 4 servings*

Lasagna Supreme

 8 ounces uncooked lasagna noodles
½ pound mild Italian sausage, casings removed
½ pound ground beef
 1 medium onion, chopped
 2 cloves garlic, minced
 1 can (about 14 ounces) whole tomatoes, undrained and chopped
 1 can (6 ounces) tomato paste
 2 teaspoons dried basil
 1 teaspoon dried marjoram
 1 can (4 ounces) sliced mushrooms, drained
 2 eggs
 2 cups (16 ounces) cream-style cottage cheese
¾ cup grated Parmesan cheese, divided
 2 tablespoons dried parsley flakes
½ teaspoon salt
½ teaspoon black pepper
 2 cups (8 ounces) shredded Cheddar cheese
 3 cups (12 ounces) shredded mozzarella cheese

1. Cook lasagna noodles according to package directions; drain.

2. Meanwhile, brown sausage, ground beef, onion and garlic in large skillet over medium-high heat, stirring to break up meat; drain fat. Add tomatoes with liquid, tomato paste, basil and marjoram. Reduce heat to low. Cover; simmer 15 minutes, stirring often. Stir in mushrooms; set aside.

3. Preheat oven to 375°F. Beat eggs in large bowl; add cottage cheese, ½ cup Parmesan, parsley flakes, salt and pepper. Mix well.

4. Place half of noodles in bottom of greased 13×9-inch baking pan. Spread half of cottage cheese mixture over noodles, then half of meat mixture, half of Cheddar and half of mozzarella. Repeat layers. Top with remaining ¼ cup Parmesan.

5. Bake lasagna 40 to 45 minutes or until hot and bubbly. Let stand 10 minutes before cutting. *Makes 8 to 10 servings*

This lasagna can be assembled, covered and refrigerated up to 2 days in advance. Bake, uncovered, in preheated 375°F oven 60 minutes or until hot and bubbly.

Super Salads

They broke bread in their homes and ate together with glad and sincere hearts.   *Acts 2:46 NIV*

Very Verde Green Bean Salad

 1 **tablespoon olive oil**
 1 **pound fresh green beans**
 ½ **cup water**
 ½ **teaspoon salt**
 ½ **teaspoon black pepper**
 ½ **cup ORTEGA® Salsa Verde**
 2 **tablespoons ORTEGA® Garden Vegetable Salsa**

Heat oil in large skillet over medium heat. When oil begins to shimmer, add green beans; toss lightly in oil. Heat about 3 minutes, tossing to coat beans well.

Add water, salt and pepper carefully. Cover; cook 5 minutes or until beans are tender. Add salsas; toss to coat beans evenly. Heat 1 or 2 minutes to warm salsas. Refrigerate or serve at room temperature.   *Makes 4 servings*

Prep Time: 5 minutes
Start to Finish: 15 minutes

Roasted Vegetable Salad with Capers and Walnuts

Salad
- **1 pound small Brussels sprouts**
- **1 pound small Yukon Gold potatoes**
- **¼ teaspoon salt**
- **¼ teaspoon black pepper**
- **¼ teaspoon dried rosemary**
- **3 tablespoons olive oil**
- **1 large red bell pepper, cut into bite-size chunks**
- **¼ cup walnuts, coarsely chopped**
- **2 tablespoons capers**

Dressing
- **2 tablespoons extra-virgin olive oil**
- **1½ tablespoons white wine vinegar**
- **Salt and black pepper to taste**

1. Preheat oven to 400°F. For salad, wash, trim and pat dry Brussels sprouts. Slash bottoms. Scrub and pat dry potatoes; cut into halves.

2. Place Brussels sprouts and potatoes in shallow roasting pan; sprinkle with salt, black pepper and rosemary. Drizzle with olive oil; toss to coat. Roast 20 minutes. Stir in bell pepper; roast 15 minutes or until vegetables are tender. Transfer to large serving bowl; stir in walnuts and capers.

3. For dressing, whisk oil, vinegar, salt and black pepper in small bowl until well blended. Pour over salad; toss to coat. Serve at room temperature.

Makes 6 to 8 servings

To bring this salad as a potluck dish, prepare in advance. Cover and refrigerate up to one day. Serve at room temperature.

Cran-Raspberry Gelatin Salad

2 cups boiling water
1 package (4-serving size) cranberry gelatin
1 package (4-serving size) raspberry gelatin
1 can (16 ounces) jellied cranberry sauce
1 tablespoon lemon juice
4 cups frozen raspberries, thawed and drained
1 cup chopped walnuts

1. Coat 1 (2-quart) ring mold with nonstick cooking spray; place on baking sheet.

2. Combine boiling water and gelatins in large bowl; stir until dissolved. Melt cranberry sauce in medium saucepan over low heat about 5 minutes. Add cranberry sauce and lemon juice to gelatin mixture; whisk until smooth. Fold in raspberries and walnuts. Pour into prepared mold. Cover and refrigerate about 6 hours or until firm.

Makes 12 servings

Potato, Cucumber and Dill Salad

3 large IDAHO® Potatoes, unpeeled and thinly sliced
¼ cup rice wine vinegar
1½ tablespoons Dijon mustard
¼ cup canola or vegetable oil
½ cup chopped fresh dill, *or* 1 tablespoon dried whole dill weed
½ teaspoon salt
1 large cucumber, unpeeled and thinly sliced

1. Place potato slices in a 9-inch square microwave-safe baking dish; cover with microwaveable plastic wrap and microwave on HIGH 9 to 11 minutes or until tender, stirring gently every 3 minutes.

2. Combine vinegar, mustard, oil, dill and salt in a small jar. Cover tightly and shake vigorously. Pour vinegar mixture over potatoes. Cover and refrigerate until chilled. Gently mix in sliced cucumber before serving.

Makes 4 servings

A baked potato is done when it reaches an internal temperature of 210°F.

Cran-Raspberry Gelatin Salad

Nine-Layer Salad

6 cups baby spinach, packed
1½ cups grape tomatoes
2 cups pattypan squash, halved crosswise
1 cup peas, blanched
4 ounces baby corn, halved lengthwise
2 cups baby carrots, blanched and halved lengthwise
1 cup peppercorn-ranch salad dressing
1 cup shredded Cheddar cheese
4 strips bacon

1. Layer spinach, tomatoes, squash, peas, corn and carrots in 4-quart glass bowl. Pour dressing over salad; spread evenly. Top with cheese. Cover and refrigerate 4 hours.

2. Cook bacon in medium skillet over medium-high heat until crispy. Crumble and sprinkle over top of salad. *Makes 7 servings*

Southwest Pasta Salad

12 ounces tri-color rotini
1 can (15 ounces) kidney beans, drained and rinsed
1 can (11 ounces) whole kernel corn, drained
⅓ cup chopped red pepper
⅓ cup chopped green pepper
3 green onions, chopped
1 cup oil-free Italian salad dressing
2 to 3 tablespoons salad seasoning
¾ cup grated Cheddar cheese

Prepare pasta according to package directions; rinse with cold water and drain. In large bowl combine pasta, beans, corn, red and green pepper and onion. Mix salad dressing with salad seasoning and add to pasta mixture. Add cheese and toss. Refrigerate 3 to 4 hours to blend flavors. Add additional salad dressing if desired.

Makes 6 servings

Favorite recipe from **North Dakota Wheat Commission**

Sesame Rice Salad

1 can (15 ounces) mandarin orange segments, undrained
1 teaspoon ground ginger
2 cups MINUTE® Brown Rice, uncooked
½ cup Asian sesame salad dressing
3 green onions, thinly sliced
1 can (8 ounces) sliced water chestnuts, drained and chopped
½ cup sliced celery

Drain oranges, reserving liquid. Add enough water to reserved liquid to measure 1¾ cups. Stir in ginger. Prepare rice according to package directions, substituting 1¾ cups orange liquid for water. Refrigerate cooked rice 30 minutes. Add dressing, onions, water chestnuts and celery; mix lightly. Gently stir in oranges.

Makes 4 servings

Loaded, Baked Potato Salad

4 pounds IDAHO® potatoes, peeled
1 pound bacon, crisply cooked, and chopped into
     ½-inch pieces (fat reserved, if desired)
4 ounces unsalted butter, softened
½ cup chopped green onions
2 cups grated or shredded Cheddar cheese
1½ cups sour cream (regular or low-fat)
1 tablespoon black pepper
1 teaspoon salt

1. Cook whole potatoes in boiling, unsalted water until tender. Refrigerate until chilled, then chop into 1-inch pieces.

2. Transfer the potatoes to a large bowl along with the remaining ingredients and thoroughly combine. Add some of the reserved bacon fat if desired.

3. Chill at least 2 hours before serving. Adjust the seasoning prior to serving.

Makes 2 quarts

Note: Any condiments or toppings typically added to a loaded baked potato may be used for this recipe.

Roasted Sweet Potato Salad

2 pounds sweet potatoes or yams, peeled and cut into ½-inch cubes
¾ cup HELLMANN'S® or BEST FOODS® Canola Cholesterol Free
    Mayonnaise, divided
1 medium Granny Smith apple, cored and cut into ¼-inch cubes
½ cup dried cranberries

1. Preheat oven to 400°F.

2. In medium bowl, toss potatoes with 2 tablespoons HELLMANN'S® or BEST FOODS® Canola Cholesterol Free Mayonnaise. On baking sheet, evenly spread potatoes.

3. Bake, stirring once, 30 minutes or until potatoes are tender; cool completely.

4. In large bowl, combine potatoes, apple, cranberries and remaining Mayonnaise; toss to coat. Chill, if desired. *Makes 10 servings*

Prep Time: 20 minutes
Chill Time: 30 minutes

For an extra special twist, add Sweetened Pecans. In 12-inch nonstick skillet, cook 1 cup chopped pecans with 6 tablespoons sugar, stirring constantly, 5 minutes or until sugar browns. Spread pecan mixture onto greased aluminum foil. Let cool. Break into bite-size pieces and add to salad just before serving.

Fiesta Pasta Salad

12 ounces tricolor rotini pasta
 1 cup ORTEGA® Garden Vegetable Salsa
¼ cup mayonnaise
 1 cup frozen whole-kernel corn, thawed
 1 cup JOAN OF ARC® Black Beans, drained
 2 tablespoons ORTEGA® Diced Jalapeños
 3 green onions, diced
½ cup chopped fresh cilantro

Cook pasta according to package directions. Cool.

Combine pasta, salsa, mayonnaise, corn, beans, jalapeños, green onions and cilantro in large bowl; mix well. Refrigerate at least 30 minutes before serving.

Makes 6 to 8 servings

Prep Time: 5 minutes
Start to Finish: 45 minutes

Pesto Rice Salad

2 cups MINUTE® White Rice, uncooked
1 package (7 ounces) basil pesto sauce
1 cup cherry tomatoes, halved
8 ounces whole-milk mozzarella cheese, cut into ½-inch cubes
⅓ cup shredded Parmesan cheese
Toasted pine nuts (optional)

Prepare rice according to package directions. Place in large bowl. Let stand 10 minutes. Add pesto sauce; mix well. Gently stir in tomatoes and cheese. Serve warm or cover and refrigerate until ready to serve. Sprinkle with pine nuts, if desired.

Makes 6 servings

To toast pine nuts, spread in single layer in heavy-bottomed skillet. Cook over medium heat 1 to 2 minutes, stirring frequently, until nuts are lightly browned. Remove from skillet immediately. Cool before using.

Pounceole Salad

1 can (20 ounces) hominy
2 teaspoons water
1 can (15 ounces) JOAN OF ARC® Kidney Beans or pinto beans, drained,
    rinsed
1 can (15 ounces) yellow corn, drained
½ cup diced red bell pepper
½ cup diced red onion
3 tablespoons ORTEGA® Diced Green Chiles
½ teaspoon salt
½ teaspoon black pepper
½ cup ORTEGA® Original Salsa, Medium

Pour hominy into skillet; add water. Cook over low heat; separate hominy with wooden spoon. Drain well. Place into large bowl. Add beans, corn, bell pepper, onion, chiles, salt and black pepper. Toss to combine well. Stir in salsa. Serve at room temperature or refrigerate up to 24 hours.   *Makes 6 to 8 servings*

Variation: For additional color and an intriguing flavor, substitute cooked and shelled edamame for the beans.

Prep Time: 5 minutes
Start to Finish: 20 minutes

Tapioca Fruit Salad

1½ cups coconut milk
1 cup milk
¾ cup sugar, divided
2 eggs, beaten
¼ cup water
3 tablespoons quick-cooking tapioca
½ teaspoon vanilla
Pinch salt
2 cups fresh pineapple chunks
2 cups quartered fresh strawberries
1 cup diced mango
1 cup fresh blueberries
1 cup fresh blackberries
Grated peel of 1 lime
2 tablespoons lime juice

1. Mix coconut milk, milk, ½ cup sugar, eggs, water, tapioca, vanilla and salt in medium saucepan. Let stand 5 minutes. Cook over medium heat, stirring, until full boil. Remove from heat. Cool 30 minutes. (Pudding thickens as it cools.)

2. Spoon into individual dessert bowls. Combine pineapple, strawberries, mango, blueberries and blackberries in large bowl. Stir in remaining ¼ cup sugar, lime peel and juice; mix well. Spoon over tapioca.

3. Cover; refrigerate 2 to 3 hours before serving.   *Makes 8 servings*

Seafood Feasts

The Family Table
Be known to us in breaking bread, but do not
then depart; Saviour, abide with us, and spread
Thy table in our heart. *James Montgomery*

Tuna Tomato Casserole

2 cans (6 ounces each) tuna, drained
1 cup mayonnaise
1 small onion, finely chopped
¼ teaspoon salt
¼ teaspoon black pepper
1 package (12 ounces) uncooked wide egg noodles
8 to 10 plum tomatoes, sliced ¼ inch thick
1 cup (4 ounces) shredded Cheddar or mozzarella cheese

1. Preheat oven to 375°F.

2. Combine tuna, mayonnaise, onion, salt and pepper in medium bowl; mix well.

3. Cook noodles according to package directions. Drain and return to saucepan. Stir tuna mixture into noodles until well blended.

4. Layer half of noodle mixture, half of tomatoes and half of cheese in 13×9-inch baking dish. Press down slightly. Repeat layers.

5. Bake 20 minutes or until cheese is melted and casserole is heated through.

Makes 6 servings

Lemon Shrimp

  1 package (12 ounces) uncooked egg noodles
½ cup (1 stick) butter, softened
  2 pounds medium cooked shrimp
  3 tomatoes, chopped
  1 cup shredded carrots
  1 cup chicken broth
  1 can (4 ounces) sliced mushrooms, drained
  2 tablespoons lemon juice
  2 cloves garlic, chopped
½ teaspoon celery seed
¼ teaspoon black pepper

1. Preheat oven to 350°F. Cook noodles according to package directions. Drain; toss with butter in large bowl until butter is melted and noodles are evenly coated. Stir in remaining ingredients. Transfer to 3-quart casserole.

2. Bake 15 to 20 minutes or until heated through.   *Makes 8 servings*

Baked Red Snappers with Veg•All®

  2 pounds red snapper
  1 small onion, minced
½ green pepper, minced
  1 jalapeño (with seeds), minced
½ cup black olives, sliced
  4 garlic cloves, minced
  1 can (15 ounces) VEG•ALL® Original Mixed Vegetables, drained
  2 cups cooked rice
½ teaspoon salt
¼ teaspoon pepper

Preheat oven to 400°F.

Lightly grease oven-proof casserole dish.

Place snapper in casserole dish without crowding.

In medium bowl, mix onion, green pepper, jalapeño, black olives and garlic.

Stir in Veg•All, rice, salt and pepper.

Lightly stuff cavities of snapper with filling. Place any remaining filling around snapper.

Bake 20 minutes.   Makes 4 servings

Lemon Shrimp

Crab-Artichoke Casserole

  8 ounces uncooked small shell pasta
  2 tablespoons butter
  6 green onions, chopped
  2 tablespoons all-purpose flour
  1 cup half-and-half
  1 teaspoon dry mustard
  ½ teaspoon ground red pepper
     Salt and black pepper
  ½ cup (2 ounces) shredded Swiss cheese, divided
  1 package (about 8 ounces) imitation crabmeat
  1 can (about 14 ounces) artichoke hearts, drained and cut
     into bite-size pieces

1. Preheat oven to 350°F. Grease 2-quart casserole. Cook pasta according to package directions; drain and set aside.

2. Melt butter in large saucepan over medium heat. Add green onions; cook and stir about 2 minutes. Add flour; cook and stir 2 minutes. Gradually add half-and-half, whisking constantly until mixture begins to thicken. Whisk in mustard and red pepper; season to taste with salt and black pepper. Remove from heat; stir in ¼ cup cheese until melted.

3. Combine crabmeat, artichokes and pasta in prepared casserole. Add sauce mixture; stir until blended. Top with remaining ¼ cup cheese. Bake about 40 minutes or until hot, bubbly and lightly browned. *Makes 6 servings*

Creamy Alfredo Seafood Lasagna

  1 jar (1 pound) RAGÚ® Cheesy!® Classic Alfredo Sauce, divided
  1 pound imitation crabmeat, separated into bite-sized pieces
  1 container (15 ounces) ricotta cheese
  2 cups shredded mozzarella cheese (about 8 ounces), divided
  1 small onion, chopped
 12 lasagna noodles, cooked and drained
  2 tablespoons grated Parmesan cheese

1. Preheat oven to 350°F. In medium bowl, combine ½ cup Ragú Cheesy! Classic Alfredo Sauce, crabmeat, ricotta cheese, 1½ cups mozzarella cheese and onion; set aside.

continued on page 86

Creamy Alfredo Seafood Lasagna, continued

2. In 13×9-inch baking dish, spread ½ cup Pasta Sauce. Arrange 4 lasagna noodles, then top with ½ of ricotta mixture; repeat layers, ending with noodles. Top with remaining ½ cup sauce.

3. Cover with aluminum foil and bake 40 minutes. Remove foil and sprinkle with remaining ½ cup mozzarella cheese and Parmesan cheese. Bake an additional 10 minutes or until cheeses are melted. Let stand 10 minutes before serving.

Makes 8 servings

Prep Time: 25 minutes
Cook Time: 50 minutes

Crustless Salmon & Broccoli Quiche

¼ **cup chopped green onions**
3 **eggs**
¼ **cup plain yogurt**
2 **teaspoons all-purpose flour**
1 **teaspoon dried basil**
⅛ **teaspoon salt**
⅛ **teaspoon black pepper**
¾ **cup frozen broccoli florets, thawed and drained**
⅓ **cup (3 ounces) drained and flaked water-packed boneless skinless**
    canned salmon
2 **tablespoons grated Parmesan cheese**
1 **plum tomato, thinly sliced**
¼ **cup fresh bread crumbs**

1. Preheat oven to 375°F. Spray 6-cup casserole or 9-inch deep-dish pie plate with nonstick cooking spray.

2. Combine green onions, eggs, yogurt, flour, basil, salt and pepper in medium bowl until well blended. Stir in broccoli, salmon and cheese. Spread evenly in prepared casserole. Top with tomato slices and sprinkle with bread crumbs.

3. Bake, uncovered, 20 to 25 minutes or until knife inserted into center comes out clean. Let stand 5 minutes. Cut in half before serving.

Makes 4 servings

Surimi Seafood-Zucchini Frittata with Fresh Tomato Sauce

2 tablespoons vegetable oil
1 zucchini, thinly sliced
½ cup chopped onion
¼ cup chopped green bell pepper
3 eggs
6 egg whites
2 teaspoons finely chopped fresh basil *or* ½ teaspoon dried basil
½ teaspoon salt (optional)
¼ teaspoon black pepper
6 ounces crab or lobster-flavored surimi seafood, chunk style
2 tablespoons butter or margarine
3 cups chunky tomato sauce

Preheat oven to 375°F. Heat oil in 10-inch heavy ovenproof skillet over medium heat. Add zucchini, onion and green pepper; cook 5 minutes, stirring often. Place in medium bowl; set aside to cool slightly. In large bowl, beat eggs and egg whites with basil, salt and black pepper until well blended. Add zucchini mixture and surimi seafood; stir well. Meanwhile, melt butter in same skillet over medium heat, swirling skillet to coat evenly with butter. Pour in egg-surimi seafood mixture and place skillet on middle shelf of oven. Bake 12 to 15 minutes, or until eggs are set throughout. Loosen around edges with metal spatula; cut into wedges. Serve hot with ½ cup tomato sauce over each frittata slice. *Makes 6 servings*

Favorite recipe from **National Fisheries Institute**

Surimi Seafood-Zucchini Frittata with Fresh Tomato Sauce

Shrimp Primavera Pot Pie

1 can (10¾ ounces) condensed cream of shrimp soup, undiluted
1 package (12 ounces) frozen medium raw shrimp, peeled
2 packages (1 pound each) frozen mixed vegetables, such as green beans, potatoes, onions and red bell peppers, thawed and drained
1 teaspoon dried dill weed
¼ teaspoon salt
¼ teaspoon black pepper
1 package (11 ounces) refrigerated breadstick dough

1. Preheat oven to 400°F.

2. Heat soup in medium ovenproof skillet over medium-high heat 1 minute. Add shrimp; cook and stir 3 minutes or until shrimp begin to thaw. Stir in vegetables, dill, salt and pepper; mix well. Reduce heat to medium-low; cook and stir 3 minutes.

3. Unwrap breadstick dough; separate into 8 strips. Twist strips and arrange attractively over shrimp mixture in crisscross pattern, cutting to fit skillet. Press ends of dough lightly to edge of skillet to secure.

4. Bake 18 minutes or until crust is golden brown and shrimp mixture is hot and bubbly. *Makes 4 to 6 servings*

Prep and Cook Time: 30 minutes

Shrimp Primavera Pot Pie

Mediterranean-Style Tuna Noodle Casserole

 1 tablespoon extra-virgin olive oil
 4 cloves garlic, minced
 2 large onions, chopped (1½ cups)
12 ounces mushrooms, chopped (4 cups)
 2 large tomatoes, chopped
 1 red bell pepper, diced (1 cup)
 1 green bell pepper, diced (1 cup)
 1 cup chopped fresh cilantro leaves *or* ¼ cup dried oregano leaves
 2 tablespoons dried marjoram or oregano leaves
 1 to 2 teaspoons ground red pepper
 1 pound JARLSBERG LITE™ cheese, shredded (4 cups)
 1 (16-ounce) can black-eyed peas, rinsed and drained
 2 (7-ounce) cans tuna, drained and flaked
 6 ounces cooked pasta (tricolor rotelle, bows or macaroni)

Preheat oven to 350°F. Heat oil in large skillet; sauté garlic until golden. Add onions; sauté until transparent, about 2 minutes on medium-high heat.

Add mushrooms, tomatoes and bell peppers; cook and stir 3 to 5 minutes or until mushrooms begin to brown. Add cilantro, marjoram and ground red pepper.

Toss with cheese, peas, tuna and pasta. Pour into greased baking dish. Bake, covered, 45 minutes or until cooked through.   *Makes 6 to 8 servings*

Serving Suggestion: Serve with crusty bread and homemade coleslaw.

Salmon Casserole

2 tablespoons butter
2 cups sliced mushrooms
1½ cups chopped carrots
1 cup frozen peas
1 cup chopped celery
½ cup chopped onion
½ cup chopped red bell pepper
1 tablespoon chopped fresh parsley
1 clove garlic, minced
1 teaspoon salt
½ teaspoon black pepper
½ teaspoon dried basil
4 cups cooked rice
1 can (14 ounces) red salmon, drained and flaked
1 can (10¾ ounces) condensed cream of mushroom soup, undiluted
2 cups (8 ounces) shredded Cheddar or American cheese
½ cup sliced black olives

1. Preheat oven to 350°F. Spray 2-quart casserole with nonstick cooking spray.

2. Melt butter in large skillet or Dutch oven over medium heat. Add mushrooms, carrots, peas, celery, onion, bell pepper, parsley, garlic, salt, black pepper and basil; cook and stir 10 minutes or until vegetables are tender. Add rice, salmon, soup and cheese; mix well.

3. Transfer to prepared casserole; sprinkle with olives. Bake 30 minutes or until hot and bubbly. *Makes 6 to 8 servings*

Red salmon, also known as sockeye, has firm, deep red flesh and can be found in the Pacific Ocean.

Paella

¼ cup FILIPPO BERIO® Olive Oil
1 pound boneless skinless chicken breasts, cut into 1-inch strips
½ pound Italian sausage links, cut into 1-inch slices
1 onion, chopped
3 cloves garlic, minced
2 (14½-ounce) cans chicken broth
2 cups uncooked long grain white rice
1 (8-ounce) bottle clam juice
1 (2-ounce) jar chopped pimientos, drained
2 bay leaves
1 teaspoon salt
¼ teaspoon saffron threads, crumbled (optional)
1 pound raw shrimp, shelled and deveined
1 (16-ounce) can whole tomatoes, drained
1 (10-ounce) package frozen peas, thawed
12 littleneck clams, scrubbed
¼ cup water
Fresh herb sprig (optional)

Preheat oven to 350°F. In large skillet, heat olive oil over medium heat until hot. Add chicken; cook and stir 8 to 10 minutes or until brown on all sides. Remove with slotted spoon; set aside. Add sausage to skillet; cook and stir 8 to 10 minutes or until brown. Remove with slotted spoon; set aside. Add onion and garlic to skillet; cook and stir 5 to 7 minutes or until onion is tender. Transfer chicken, sausage, onion and garlic to large casserole.

Add chicken broth, rice, clam juice, pimientos, bay leaves, salt and saffron, if desired, to chicken mixture. Cover; bake 30 minutes. Add shrimp, tomatoes and peas; stir well. Cover; bake an additional 15 minutes or until rice is tender, liquid is absorbed and shrimp are opaque. Remove bay leaves.

Meanwhile, combine clams and water in stockpot or large saucepan. Cover; cook over medium heat 5 to 10 minutes or until clams open; remove clams immediately as they open. Discard any clams with unopened shells. Place clams on top of paella. Garnish with herb sprig, if desired. *Makes 4 to 6 servings*

Crunchy Veg•All® Tuna Casserole

  2 cups cooked medium egg noodles
  1 can (15 ounces) VEG•ALL® Original Mixed Vegetables, drained
  1 can (12 ounces) solid white tuna in water, drained
  1 can (10¾ ounces) cream of celery soup, undiluted
1¼ cups whole milk
  ½ cup sour cream
  1 tablespoon chopped fresh dill
  1 cup crushed sour cream & onion potato chips

Combine all ingredients except potato chips in greased 1½-quart casserole dish.

Microwave, uncovered, on High for 10 to 12 minutes or until very thick. Let cool for 10 minutes.

Top with crushed potato chips and serve. *Makes 4 to 6 servings*

Shrimp Creole

  2 tablespoons olive oil
1½ cups chopped green bell peppers
  1 medium onion, chopped
  ⅔ cup chopped celery
  2 cloves garlic, finely chopped
  1 cup uncooked rice
  1 can (about 14 ounces) diced tomatoes, drained and liquid reserved
  2 teaspoons hot pepper sauce, or to taste
  1 teaspoon dried oregano
  ¾ teaspoon salt
  ½ teaspoon dried thyme
    Black pepper
  1 pound medium raw shrimp, peeled and deveined
  1 tablespoon chopped fresh parsley (optional)

1. Preheat oven to 325°F. Heat oil in large skillet over medium-high heat. Add bell peppers, onion, celery and garlic; cook and stir 5 minutes or until vegetables are tender.

2. Reduce heat to medium. Add rice; cook and stir 5 minutes. Add tomatoes, hot pepper sauce, oregano, salt, thyme and black pepper to skillet; stir until well blended. Pour reserved tomato liquid into measuring cup. Add enough water to measure 1¾ cups; add to skillet. Cook and stir 2 minutes.

3. Transfer mixture to 2½-quart casserole. Stir in shrimp. Bake, covered, 55 minutes or until rice is tender and liquid is absorbed. Garnish with parsley.

Makes 4 to 6 servings

SUNDAY SUPPERS

SUNDAY SUPPERS

Table of Contents

98 ✳ *Soups & Stews*

118 ✳ *Savory Breads*

136 ✳ *Main Dishes*

158 ✳ *On the Side*

174 ✳ *Delicious Desserts*

Soups & Stews

Fresh Lime and Black Bean Soup

2 cans (about 15 ounces each) black beans, undrained
1 can (about 14 ounces) chicken broth
1½ cups chopped onions
1½ teaspoons chili powder
¾ teaspoon ground cumin
¼ teaspoon garlic powder
⅛ to ¼ teaspoon red pepper flakes
½ cup sour cream
2 tablespoons extra-virgin olive oil
2 tablespoons chopped fresh cilantro
1 medium lime, cut into wedges

Slow Cooker Directions

1. Coat slow cooker with nonstick cooking spray. Add beans, broth, onions, chili powder, cumin, garlic powder and red pepper flakes. Cover; cook on LOW 7 hours or on HIGH 3½ hours or until onions are very soft.

2. Process 1 cup soup mixture in blender until smooth and return to slow cooker. Stir and check consistency; repeat with additional 1 cup soup as needed. Let stand 15 to 20 minutes before serving.

3. Ladle soup into bowls. Divide sour cream, oil, and cilantro evenly among servings. Squeeze juice from lime wedges over each. *Makes 4 servings*

Prep Time: 10 minutes
Cook Time: 7 hours (LOW) or 3½ hours (HIGH)

Louisiana Gumbo

  2 cups MINUTE® White Rice, uncooked
  2 tablespoons butter
  2 tablespoons all-purpose flour
  ½ cup chopped onion
  ½ cup chopped celery
  ½ cup chopped green bell pepper
  1 clove garlic, minced
  1 package (14 ounces) smoked turkey sausage, sliced
  1 can (14½ ounces) diced tomatoes
  1 can (13¾ ounces) condensed chicken broth
  1 package (10 ounces) frozen sliced okra, thawed*
  1 tablespoon Cajun seasoning
  ¼ teaspoon dried thyme
  ½ pound shrimp, peeled, deveined
  Salt and black pepper, to taste

*Or substitute 1 package (10 ounces) frozen cut green beans.

Prepare rice according to package directions. Melt butter in large skillet over medium-high heat. Stir in flour; cook and stir until light golden brown, about 5 minutes. Add onions, celery, bell pepper and garlic; cook 2 to 3 minutes or until tender. Stir in sausage, tomatoes, broth, okra, seasoning and thyme; cover. Simmer 5 minutes, stirring occasionally. Add shrimp; cook 5 minutes or until shrimp are pink. Season with salt and pepper to taste. Serve with rice. *Makes 6 servings*

Pizza Soup

  2 cans (about 14 ounces each) stewed tomatoes with
      Italian seasonings, undrained
  2 cups beef broth
  1 cup sliced mushrooms
  1 small onion, chopped
  1 tablespoon tomato paste
  ¼ teaspoon salt
  ¼ teaspoon black pepper
  ½ pound turkey Italian sausage, casings removed
  Shredded mozzarella cheese

continued on page 102

Pizza Soup, continued

Slow Cooker Directions

1. Combine tomatoes with juice, broth, mushrooms, onion, tomato paste, salt and pepper in 3½- to 4½-quart slow cooker.

2. Shape sausage into marble-size balls. Gently stir into soup mixture. Cover; cook on LOW 6 to 7 hours. Sprinkle with cheese. *Makes 4 servings*

Prep Time: 10 minutes
Cook Time: 6 to 7 hours

Hearty Chicken Chili

    1 medium onion, finely chopped
    1 small jalapeño pepper,* cored, seeded and minced
    1 clove garlic, minced
 1½ teaspoons chili powder
   ¾ teaspoon salt
   ½ teaspoon black pepper
   ½ teaspoon ground cumin
   ½ teaspoon dried oregano
   ¼ teaspoon red pepper flakes (optional)
 1½ pounds boneless skinless chicken thighs, cut into 1-inch pieces
    2 cans (about 15 ounces each) hominy, rinsed and drained
    1 can (about 15 ounces) pinto beans, rinsed and drained
    1 cup chicken broth
    1 tablespoon all-purpose flour (optional)
      Chopped fresh parsley or fresh cilantro (optional)

*Jalapeño peppers can sting and irritate the skin, so wear rubber gloves when handling peppers and do not touch eyes.

Slow Cooker Directions

1. Combine onion, jalapeño, garlic, chili powder, salt, pepper, cumin, oregano and red pepper flakes, if desired, in slow cooker.

2. Add chicken, hominy, beans and broth. Stir well to combine. Cover; cook on LOW 7 hours.

3. If thicker gravy is desired, combine 1 tablespoon flour and 3 tablespoons cooking liquid in small bowl. Add to slow cooker. Cover; cook on HIGH 10 minutes or until thickened. Serve in bowls and garnish with parsley. *Makes 6 servings*

Prep Time: 15 minutes
Cook Time: 7 hours (LOW), plus 10 minutes (HIGH)

Italian Mushroom Soup

1½ **cups boiling water**
½ **cup dried porcini mushrooms (about ½ ounce)**
1 **tablespoon olive oil**
2 **cups chopped onions**
8 **ounces sliced button or cremini mushrooms**
2 **cloves garlic, minced**
¼ **teaspoon dried thyme**
¼ **cup all-purpose flour**
4 **cups chicken or vegetable broth**
½ **cup whipping cream**
½ **teaspoon black pepper**

1. Combine boiling water and porcini mushrooms in small bowl; let stand 15 to 20 minutes or until mushrooms are tender.

2. Meanwhile, heat oil in large saucepan over medium heat. Add onions; cook 5 minutes or until translucent, stirring occasionally. Add cremini mushrooms, garlic and thyme; cook 8 minutes, stirring occasionally. Add flour; cook and stir 1 minute. Stir in broth.

3. Drain porcini mushrooms, reserving liquid. Chop mushrooms; add mushrooms and reserved liquid to saucepan. Bring to a boil over high heat. Reduce heat; simmer 10 minutes. Stir in cream and pepper. Simmer 5 minutes or until heated through. Serve immediately. *Makes 6 to 8 servings*

 Tip Dried porcini mushrooms (also known as cèpes) are tan to pale brown in color. They have a pungent, woodsy flavor. While button mushrooms are white to pale tan in color. They have a smooth texture and mild flavor.

Jerk Pork and Sweet Potato Stew

  2 tablespoons all-purpose flour
  ¼ teaspoon salt
  ¼ teaspoon black pepper
1¼ pounds pork shoulder, cut into bite-size pieces
  2 tablespoons vegetable oil
  1 large sweet potato, peeled and diced
  1 cup corn
  ¼ cup minced green onions, divided
  1 clove garlic, minced
  ½ medium scotch bonnet chile or jalapeño pepper,* cored, seeded and minced
  ⅛ teaspoon ground allspice
  1 cup chicken broth
  1 tablespoon lime juice

Scotch bonnet chiles and jalapeño peppers can sting and irritate the skin, so wear rubber gloves when handling and do not touch your eyes.

Slow Cooker Directions

1. Combine flour, salt and black pepper in large resealable food storage bag. Add pork; shake well to coat. Heat oil in large skillet over medium heat. Working in batches, add pork in single layer and brown on all sides, about 5 minutes. Transfer to 4- or 5-quart slow cooker.

2. Add sweet potato, corn, 2 tablespoons green onions, garlic, chile and allspice. Stir in broth. Cover; cook on LOW 5 to 6 hours.

3. Stir in lime juice and remaining 2 tablespoons green onions.   *Makes 4 servings*

Spicy Squash & Chicken Soup

1 tablespoon vegetable oil
1 small onion, finely chopped
1 stalk celery, finely chopped
2 cups delicata or butternut squash (1 small squash), cut into 1-inch cubes
2 cups chicken broth
1 can (about 14 ounces) diced tomatoes, undrained
1 cup chopped cooked chicken
½ teaspoon ground ginger
¼ teaspoon salt
⅛ teaspoon *each* ground cumin and black pepper
2 teaspoons fresh lime juice
1 tablespoon minced fresh cilantro (optional)

1. Heat oil in large saucepan over medium heat. Add onion and celery; cook and stir 5 minutes or just until tender. Stir in squash, broth, tomatoes, chicken, ginger, salt, cumin and pepper; mix well.

2. Cover and cook over low heat 30 minutes or until squash is tender. Stir in lime juice. Sprinkle with cilantro.   *Makes 4 servings*

Variation: For an extra-spicy soup, use diced tomatoes with chiles.

Baked Potato Soup

 ¼ **cup (½ stick) butter or margarine**
 ¼ **cup chopped onion**
 ¼ **cup all-purpose flour**
 1 **can (14½ fluid ounces) chicken broth**
 1 **can (12 fluid ounces) NESTLÉ® CARNATION® Evaporated Milk**
 2 **large or 3 medium baking potatoes, baked or microwaved**
   Cooked and crumbled bacon (optional)
   Shredded Cheddar cheese (optional)
   Sliced green onions (optional)

Melt butter in large saucepan over medium heat. Add onion; cook, stirring occasionally, for 1 to 2 minutes or until tender. Stir in flour. Gradually stir in broth and evaporated milk. Scoop potato pulp from 1 potato (reserve potato skin); mash. Add pulp to broth mixture. Cook over medium heat, stirring occasionally, until mixture comes to a boil. Dice remaining potato skin and potato(es); add to soup. Heat through. Season with salt and ground black pepper. Top each serving with bacon, cheese and green onions, if desired.   *Makes 4 servings*

Variation: For a different twist to this recipe, omit the bacon, Cheddar cheese and green onions. Cook 2 tablespoons shredded carrot with the onion and add ¼ teaspoon dried dill to the soup when adding the broth. Proceed as above.

Italian Hillside Garden Soup

1 tablespoon extra-virgin olive oil
1 cup chopped green bell pepper
1 cup chopped onion
½ cup sliced celery
2 cans (about 14 ounces each) chicken broth
1 can (about 14 ounces) diced tomatoes with basil, garlic and oregano, undrained
1 can (about 15 ounces) navy beans, drained and rinsed
1 medium zucchini, chopped
1 cup frozen cut green beans, thawed
¼ teaspoon garlic powder
1 package (9 ounces) refrigerated sausage- or cheese-filled tortellini pasta
3 tablespoons chopped fresh basil
   Grated Asiago or Parmesan cheese (optional)

Slow Cooker Directions

1. Heat oil in large skillet over medium-high heat. Add bell pepper, onion and celery. Cook and stir 4 minutes or until onions are translucent. Transfer to 5-quart slow cooker.

2. Add broth, tomatoes with juice, navy beans, zucchini, green beans and garlic powder. Cover; cook on LOW 7 hours or on HIGH 3½ hours.

3. Turn slow cooker to HIGH. Add tortellini and cook 20 to 25 minutes longer or until pasta is tender. Stir in basil. Garnish each serving with cheese.

Makes 6 servings

Prep Time: 15 minutes
Cook Time: 7 hours (LOW) or 3½ hours (HIGH), plus 20 minutes (HIGH)

Chorizo Chili

1 pound ground beef
8 ounces bulk raw chorizo *or* ½ package (15 ounces) raw chorizo
1 can (about 16 ounces) chili beans in chili sauce
2 cans (about 14 ounces each) zesty chili-style diced tomatoes, undrained

Slow Cooker Directions

1. Place beef and chorizo in slow cooker. Stir to break up well.

2. Stir in beans and tomatoes. Cover; cook on LOW 7 hours. Skim off and discard excess fat before serving.

Makes 6 servings

Prep Time: 5 minutes
Cook Time: 7 hours

Grilled Corn & Chicken Soup

 4 ears corn-on-the-cob, husks removed
 2 poblano peppers, halved and seeded
 1 medium onion, cut into ½-inch thick slices
 ½ cup LAWRY'S® Mesquite Marinade With Lime Juice
 3 tablespoons all-purpose flour
 2 cans (14½ ounces each) chicken broth
 1½ cups milk
 2 cups shredded cooked chicken

1. Grill vegetables, turning occasionally and brushing with LAWRY'S® Mesquite Marinade With Lime Juice, 10 minutes or until vegetables are golden brown and tender. Cool slightly, then cut corn from cob and chop peppers and onion; set aside.

2. In small bowl, whisk flour with ¼ cup broth; set aside.

3. In 4-quart saucepot, combine remaining broth, milk and vegetables. Bring to a boil over high heat, stirring occasionally. Stir in flour mixture. Bring to a boil over high heat, then reduce heat to medium-low and simmer, stirring occasionally, 5 minutes. Stir in chicken and cook 2 minutes or until heated through. Garnish, if desired, with cilantro, sour cream and lime wedges.   *Makes 6 servings*

Prep Time: 15 minutes
Cook Time: 20 minutes

Tip | To cut corn from the cob, hold the tip of an ear and stand the corn upright on its stem end in a shallow dish. Cut down the side of the cob with a utility knife, releasing kernels without cutting the cob. Repeat while rotating the ear until all kernels are removed.

Asian Beef Stew

1½ pounds beef round steak, sliced thinly across the grain
2 onions, cut into ¼-inch slices
2 stalks celery, sliced
2 carrots, peeled and sliced *or* 1 cup peeled baby carrots
1 cup sliced mushrooms
1 cup orange juice
1 cup beef broth
⅓ cup hoisin sauce
2 tablespoons cornstarch
1 to 2 teaspoons Chinese five-spice powder or curry powder
1 cup frozen peas
Hot cooked rice
Chopped fresh cilantro (optional)

Slow Cooker Directions

1. Place beef, onions, celery, carrots and mushrooms in 5-quart slow cooker.

2. Combine orange juice, broth, hoisin sauce, cornstarch and five-spice powder in small bowl. Pour into slow cooker. Cover; cook on HIGH 5 hours or until beef is tender.

3. Stir in peas. Cook 20 minutes or until peas are tender. Serve with hot cooked rice. Garnish with cilantro.   *Makes 6 servings*

Prep Time: 10 minutes
Cook Time: 5 hours, 20 minutes

Hearty Vegetable Stew

1 tablespoon olive oil
1 cup chopped onion
¾ cup chopped carrots
3 cloves garlic, minced
4 cups coarsely chopped green cabbage
3½ cups coarsely chopped red potatoes (about 3 medium)
1 teaspoon dried rosemary
1 teaspoon salt
½ teaspoon black pepper
4 cups vegetable broth
1 can (about 15 ounces) Great Northern Beans, rinsed and drained
1 can (about 14 ounces) diced tomatoes
Grated Parmesan cheese (optional)

continued on page 114

Hearty Vegetable Stew, continued

1. Heat oil in large saucepan over high heat. Add onion and carrots; cook and stir 3 minutes. Add garlic; cook and stir 1 minute.

2. Add cabbage, potatoes, rosemary, salt and pepper; cook 1 minute. Stir in broth, beans and tomatoes; bring to a boil. Reduce heat to medium-low; simmer about 15 minutes or until potatoes are tender. Sprinkle with cheese.

Makes about 7 servings

Italian Sausage Soup

Sausage Meatballs

   1 pound mild Italian sausage, casings removed
   ½ cup plain dry bread crumbs
   ¼ cup grated Parmesan cheese
   ¼ cup milk
   1 egg
   ½ teaspoon dried basil
   ½ teaspoon black pepper
   ¼ teaspoon garlic salt

Soup

   4 cups chicken broth
   1 tablespoon tomato paste
   1 clove garlic, minced
   ¼ teaspoon red pepper flakes
   ½ cup mini shell pasta*
   1 bag (10 ounces) baby spinach
   Grated Parmesan cheese

*Or use other tiny pasta, such as ditalini (mini tubes) or farfallini (mini bowties).

Slow Cooker Directions

1. Combine all meatball ingredients in large bowl. Form into marble-size balls.

2. Combine broth, tomato paste, garlic and red pepper flakes in slow cooker. Add meatballs. Cover; cook on LOW 5 to 6 hours.

3. Add pasta; cook on LOW 30 minutes or until pasta is tender. Stir in spinach. Ladle into bowls; sprinkle with cheese and serve immediately. *Makes 4 to 6 servings*

Prep Time: 15 minutes
Cook Time: 5 to 6 hours

Green Chile Chicken Soup with Tortilla Dumplings

 8 **ORTEGA® Taco Shells, broken**
½ **cup water**
⅓ **cup milk**
 2 **onions, diced, divided**
 1 **egg**
½ **teaspoon POLANER® Minced Garlic**
 1 **tablespoon olive oil**
 4 **cups chicken broth**
 2 **cups shredded cooked chicken**
 2 **tablespoons ORTEGA® Roasted Chiles**
¼ **cup vegetable oil**

Place taco shells, water, milk, 1 diced onion, egg and garlic in blender or food processor. Pulse several times to crush taco shells and blend ingredients. Pour into medium bowl; let stand 10 minutes to thicken.

Heat 1 tablespoon olive oil in saucepan over medium heat. Add remaining diced onion; cook and stir 4 minutes or until translucent. Stir in broth, chicken and chiles. Reduce heat to a simmer.

Heat ¼ cup oil in small skillet over medium heat. Form taco shell mixture into 1-inch balls. Drop into hot oil in batches. Cook dumplings about 3 minutes or until browned. Turn over and continue cooking 3 minutes longer or until browned. Remove dumplings; drain on paper towels. Add dumplings to soup just before serving.

Makes 4 to 6 servings

Prep Time: 15 minutes
Start to Finish: 30 minutes

Tip   For an even more authentic Mexican flavor, garnish the soup with fresh chopped cilantro and a squirt of lime juice.

Savory Breads

Three-Grain Bread

1 cup whole wheat flour
¾ cup all-purpose flour
1 package rapid-rise active dry yeast
1 cup milk
2 tablespoons honey
1 tablespoon olive oil
1 teaspoon salt
½ cup old-fashioned oats
¼ cup whole grain cornmeal
1 egg beaten with 1 tablespoon water (optional)
1 tablespoon old-fashioned oats for topping (optional)

1. Combine whole wheat flour, all-purpose flour and yeast in large bowl. Stir milk, honey, olive oil and salt in small saucepan over low heat until warm (110° to 120°F). Stir milk mixture into flour; beat 3 minutes with electric mixer at high speed. Mix in oats and cornmeal at low speed. If dough is too wet, add additional flour by teaspoonfuls until it begins to come together.

2. Place dough on floured surface and knead 8 minutes or until dough is smooth and elastic. Place dough in large, lightly oiled bowl; turn once to coat. Cover; let dough rise in warm place (85°F) about 1 hour or until dough is puffy and does not spring back when touched.

3. Punch dough down and shape into 8-inch long loaf. Place on baking sheet lightly dusted with cornmeal. Cover; let rise in warm place until almost doubled, about 45 minutes. Meanwhile, preheat oven to 375°F.

4. Make shallow slash down center of loaf with sharp knife. Brush lightly with egg mixture and sprinkle with oats, if desired. Bake 30 minutes or until loaf sounds hollow when tapped (internal temperature of 200°F). Remove to wire rack to cool.

Makes 1 loaf

Sage Buns

1½ **cups milk**
2 **tablespoons shortening**
3 **to 4 cups all-purpose flour, divided**
2 **tablespoons sugar**
1 **package active dry yeast**
2 **teaspoons rubbed sage**
1 **teaspoon salt**
1 **tablespoon olive oil (optional)**

1. Heat milk and shortening in small saucepan over medium heat, stirring constantly, until shortening is melted and temperature reaches 120°F to 130°F. Remove from heat.

2. Combine 2 cups flour, sugar, yeast, sage and salt in large bowl. Add milk mixture; beat vigorously 2 minutes. Add remaining flour, ¼ cup at a time, until dough begins to pull away from sides of bowl.

3. Turn dough out onto floured work surface; flatten slightly. Knead 10 minutes or until dough is smooth and elastic, adding flour, if necessary, to prevent sticking.

4. Shape dough into ball. Place in large lightly oiled bowl; turn dough over once to oil surface. Cover with towel; let rise in warm place (85°F) 1 hour or until doubled. Grease 13×9-inch pan; set aside.

5. Turn out dough onto lightly oiled surface. Divide into 24 equal pieces. Form each piece into ball. Space evenly in prepared pan. Cover with towel; let rise 45 minutes.

6. Preheat oven to 375°F. Bake 15 to 20 minutes or until golden brown. Immediately remove bread from pan and cool on wire rack. Brush tops of rolls with olive oil for soft, shiny tops, if desired. *Makes 24 rolls*

Easy Cheesy Bacon Bread

1 pound sliced bacon, chopped
1 large onion, chopped
1 large green bell pepper, chopped
½ teaspoon ground red pepper
3 cans (7½ ounces each) refrigerated buttermilk biscuits
2½ cups (10 ounces) shredded Cheddar cheese, divided
½ cup (1 stick) butter, melted

1. Preheat oven to 350°F. Spray nonstick bundt pan with nonstick cooking spray. Cook bacon in large skillet over medium heat about 4 minutes or until crisp. Remove bacon with slotted spoon to paper towels. Reserve 1 tablespoon drippings in skillet. Add onion, bell pepper and red pepper; cook and stir over medium-high heat about 10 minutes or until tender. Cool.

2. Cut biscuits into quarters. Combine biscuit pieces, bacon, onion mixture, 2 cups cheese and melted butter in large bowl; mix gently. Loosely press mixture in prepared pan.

3. Bake 30 minutes or until golden brown. Cool 5 minutes in pan on wire rack. Invert onto serving platter and sprinkle with remaining ½ cup cheese. Serve warm.

Makes 12 servings

Sonoma Dried Tomato and Vegetable Biscuits

¼ cup SONOMA® Dried Tomato Halves
2½ cups unbleached all-purpose flour
1 tablespoon sugar
2 teaspoons baking powder
2 teaspoons salt
½ teaspoon baking soda
¼ teaspoon black pepper
½ teaspoon active dry yeast
2 tablespoons warm water (110° to 115°F)
1 cup cold vegetable shortening, cut into ½-inch cubes
½ cup vegetables, cut into ¼-inch cubes (carrot, yellow squash, green bell pepper and zucchini)
2 teaspoons *each* fresh minced parsley, basil and dill *or* 1 scant teaspoon *each* dried parsley, basil and dill
1 large clove garlic, minced
¾ cup buttermilk

continued on page 124

Sonoma Dried Tomato and Vegetable Biscuits, continued

Preheat oven to 375°F. In small bowl, cover tomatoes with boiling water; set aside 10 minutes. In large bowl, mix flour, sugar, baking powder, salt, baking soda and black pepper. In another small bowl, dissolve yeast in warm water; set aside. Cut shortening into flour mixture until crumbs resemble coarse meal. Blend yeast mixture into flour mixture to form dough. Thoroughly drain and mince tomatoes; combine with vegetables, herbs and garlic. Add half the vegetable mixture and half the buttermilk to the dough; mix well and repeat with remaining vegetable mixture and buttermilk. Turn dough out onto floured surface and knead several times, adding more flour only if necessary. Pat or roll out dough to ¾-inch thickness; cut out dough with 3-inch biscuit cutter. Place biscuits, spaced 2 inches apart, on greased or parchment-lined baking sheet. Bake 20 to 24 minutes until lightly browned and cooked through.

Makes 8 biscuits

Honey Whole-Grain Bread

3 cups whole wheat flour, divided
2 cups warm (not hot) whole milk
¾ to 1 cup all-purpose flour, divided
¼ cup honey
2 tablespoons vegetable oil
1 package (¼ ounce) active dry yeast
¾ teaspoon salt

Slow Cooker Directions

1. Spray 1-quart casserole, soufflé dish or other high-sided baking pan that fits into slow cooker with nonstick cooking spray. Combine 1½ cups whole wheat flour, milk, ½ cup all-purpose flour, honey, oil, yeast and salt in large bowl. Beat with electric mixer at medium speed 2 minutes.

2. Add remaining 1½ cups whole wheat flour and ¼ cup to ½ cup all-purpose flour until dough is no longer sticky. (If mixer has difficulty mixing dough, mix in remaining flours with wooden spoon.) Transfer to prepared dish.

3. Make foil handles with strips of heavy-duty foil. Criss-cross 3 or 4 strips and place in slow cooker. Place dish on strips. Cover; cook on HIGH 3 hours or until edges are browned.

4. Use foil handles to lift dish from slow cooker. Let stand 5 minutes. Unmold on wire rack to cool.

Makes 8 to 10 servings

Good Old American White Rolls

¾ **cup milk**
¼ **cup (½ stick) butter**
 2 **eggs**
 1 **teaspoon salt**
¼ **cup sugar**
 3 **cups bread flour**
2¼ **teaspoons (1 packet) RED STAR® Active Dry Yeast or QUICK•RISE™**
     Yeast or Bread Machine Yeast

Bread Machine Method

Place room temperature ingredients in pan in order listed. Select dough cycle. Do not use the delay timer. Check dough consistency after 5 minutes of kneading, making adjustments, if necessary.

Hand-Held Mixer Method

Combine yeast, 1 cup flour, sugar and salt. Heat milk and butter to 120° to 130°F (butter does not need to melt). Combine dry mixture, milk and butter in mixing bowl on low speed. Beat 2 to 3 minutes on medium speed. Add room temperature eggs; beat 1 minute. By hand, stir in enough remaining flour to make a firm dough. Knead on floured surface 5 to 7 minutes or until smooth and elastic. Add additional flour, if necessary.

Stand Mixer Method

Combine yeast, 1 cup flour, sugar and salt. Heat milk and butter to 120° to 130°F (butter does not need to melt). Combine dry mixture, milk and butter in mixer bowl with paddle or beaters for 4 minutes on medium speed. Add room temperature eggs; beat 1 minute. Gradually add flour and knead with dough hooks 5 to 7 minutes or until smooth and elastic. Add additional flour, if necessary.

Food Processor Method

Divide milk. In a 2-cup measure, heat ¼ cup milk to 110° to 115°F; add yeast and set aside. Insert dough blade in work bowl; add bread flour, sugar and salt. Pulse to combine. Have butter, eggs and remaining ½ cup milk cold. Add cold butter, eggs and milk to yeast mixture; stir to combine. With machine running, add liquid mixture through feed tube in a steady stream only as fast as flour will absorb it. Open lid to check dough consistency. If dough is stiff and somewhat dry, add 1 teaspoon water; if soft and sticky, add 1 tablespoon flour. Check dough consistency again, making additional adjustments if necessary. Once dough forms a ball, continue processing for 10 seconds to knead dough.

Rising, Shaping and Baking

Place dough in lightly oiled bowl and turn to grease top. Cover; let rise until dough tests ripe.* Divide dough into 4 parts; divide each part into 3 pieces. For pan rolls, shape each piece into smooth ball, place in greased 9-inch cake pan. For individual rolls, place balls in greased muffin pan cups or 2 to 3 inches apart on greased baking sheet. Cover; let rise at room temperature until indentation remains when touched. Bake in preheated 375°F oven: pan rolls, 20 to 25 minutes; individual rolls, 12 to 15 minutes. If desired, lightly brush with butter. Remove from pan and cool.

Makes 1 dozen rolls

Place two fingers into the risen dough up to second knuckle and take out. If the indentations remain the dough is ripe and ready to punch down.

Thyme-Cheese Bubble Loaf

    1 cup water
    2 tablespoons vegetable oil
    1 teaspoon salt
    3 cups all-purpose flour
    1 cup (4 ounces) shredded Monterey Jack cheese
    1 teaspoon sugar
 1½ teaspoons active dry yeast
    ¼ cup chopped fresh parsley
    1 tablespoon finely chopped fresh thyme *or* ¾ teaspoon
        dried thyme
    ¼ cup (½ stick) butter, melted

Bread Machine Directions

1. Measuring carefully, place all ingredients except parsley, thyme and melted butter in bread machine pan in order specified by owner's manual. Program dough cycle setting; press start. Combine parsley and thyme in shallow bowl; set aside. Lightly grease 9×5-inch loaf pan or 1½-quart casserole dish; set aside.

2. When cycle is complete, remove dough to lightly floured surface. If necessary, knead in additional all-purpose flour to make dough easy to handle. Divide dough into 48 equal pieces. Shape each piece into smooth ball. Dip each ball into melted butter and then in herb mixture; place, in two evenly spaced layers, in prepared pan. Cover with clean towel; let rise in warm, draft-free place 45 minutes or until doubled.

3. Preheat oven to 375°F. Bake 25 to 35 minutes or until golden brown. Remove from pan; cool on wire rack.

Makes 1 loaf

Farmer-Style Sour Cream Bread

      1 cup sour cream, at room temperature
      3 tablespoons water
  2½ to 3 cups all-purpose flour, divided
      1 package active dry yeast
      2 tablespoons sugar
  1½ teaspoons salt
      ¼ teaspoon baking soda
         Vegetable oil or nonstick cooking spray
      1 tablespoon poppy or sesame seeds

1. Stir together sour cream and water in small saucepan. Heat over low heat until temperature reaches 120° to 130°F. *Do not boil.* Combine 2 cups flour, yeast, sugar, salt and baking soda in large bowl. Stir sour cream mixture into flour mixture until well blended. Turn out onto lightly floured surface. Knead about 5 minutes, adding enough remaining flour until dough is smooth and elastic.

2. Grease large baking sheet. Shape dough into ball; place on prepared sheet. Flatten into 8-inch circle. Brush top with oil. Sprinkle with poppy seeds. Invert large bowl over dough and let rise in warm place (85°F) 1 hour or until doubled.

3. Preheat oven to 350°F. Bake 22 to 27 minutes or until golden brown. Remove immediately from baking sheet; cool on wire rack.   *Makes 8 to 12 servings*

Roman Meal® Cream of Rye Bread

  1¼ teaspoons yeast
      2 cups flour
      ⅔ cup ROMAN MEAL® Cream of Rye Cereal
      2 tablespoons nonfat dry milk
      1 teaspoon salt
      2 teaspoons caraway seeds
      1 tablespoon honey
      2 teaspoons molasses
      2 tablespoons shortening
      1 cup water

Bread Machine Directions
Pour yeast to one side of inner pan. Add remaining ingredients in order. Select white bread and push "start."   *Makes 1 loaf*

Roasted Garlic Breadsticks

  1 large head garlic (about 14 to 16 cloves)
  3 tablespoons olive oil, divided
  3 tablespoons water, divided
  1 tablespoon butter or margarine, softened
  1 cup warm water (110° to 120°F)
  1 package active dry yeast
  1 teaspoon sugar
2½ to 3 cups all-purpose flour, divided
  1 teaspoon salt
  1 egg white
  1 tablespoon sesame seeds

1. Preheat oven to 350°F. Remove outer papery skin from garlic. Place garlic in 10-ounce ovenproof custard cup. Drizzle with 1 tablespoon oil and 2 tablespoons water. Cover tightly with foil. Bake 1 hour or until garlic cloves are tender. Remove foil and let cool.

2. When garlic is cool enough to handle, break into cloves. Squeeze skin until garlic pops out. Finely chop garlic cloves. Combine chopped garlic and butter in small bowl. Cover and set aside.

3. Combine warm water, yeast and sugar in large bowl; let stand 5 minutes, or until bubbly. Beat 1½ cups flour, salt and remaining 2 tablespoons oil into yeast mixture with electric mixer at low speed until blended. Increase speed to medium; beat 2 minutes. Stir in enough additional flour, about 1 cup, with wooden spoon to make soft dough.

4. Turn out onto lightly floured surface. Knead about 5 minutes, adding enough remaining flour until dough is smooth and elastic. Shape dough into ball; place in large greased bowl. Turn dough over so that top is greased. Cover with clean towel; let rise in warm place (85°F) about 1 hour or until doubled.

5. Punch down dough; knead on lightly floured surface 1 minute. Cover with towel; let rest 10 minutes. Grease 2 large baking sheets; set aside. Roll dough into 12-inch square with lightly floured rolling pin. Spread garlic mixture evenly over dough. Fold square in half. Roll dough into 14×7-inch rectangle. Cut dough crosswise into 7×1-inch strips.

6. Holding ends of each strip, twist 3 to 4 times. Place strips 2 inches apart on prepared baking sheets, pressing both ends to seal. Cover with clean towels; let rise in warm place about 30 minutes or until doubled.

7. Preheat oven to 400°F. Combine egg white and remaining 1 tablespoon water in small bowl. Brush sticks with egg white mixture; sprinkle with sesame seeds. Bake 20 to 22 minutes or until golden. Serve warm.   *Makes 12 breadsticks*

Spicy Cheese Bread

2 packages active dry yeast
1 teaspoon granulated sugar
½ cup warm water (110°F)
8¾ cups flour, divided
3 cups shredded Jarlsberg or Swiss cheese
2 tablespoons fresh chopped rosemary *or* 2 teaspoons dried rosemary
1 tablespoon salt
1 tablespoon Original TABASCO® brand Pepper Sauce
2 cups milk
4 eggs, lightly beaten

Combine yeast, sugar and warm water. Let stand 5 minutes or until foamy. Meanwhile, combine 8 cups flour, cheese, rosemary, salt and TABASCO® Sauce in large bowl. Heat milk in small saucepan until warm (120° to 130°F).

Stir milk into flour mixture. Set aside 1 tablespoon beaten egg. Add remaining eggs to flour mixture with foamy yeast mixture; stir until soft dough forms.

Turn dough out onto lightly floured surface. Knead about 5 minutes, adding enough remaining flour to make a smooth and elastic dough. Shape dough into a ball; place in large greased bowl. Cover with towel and let rise in warm place until doubled, about 1½ hours.

Grease 2 large cookie sheets. Punch down dough and divide in half. Cut each half into 3 strips and braid. Place braided loaves on greased cookie sheets. Cover and let rise in warm place until almost doubled, 30 minutes to 1 hour. Preheat oven to 375°F. Brush loaves with reserved egg. Bake about 45 minutes or until loaves sound hollow when tapped. Remove to wire racks to cool.   *Makes 2 loaves*

English Bath Buns

½ **cup warm water (100° to 110°F)**
2 **envelopes FLEISCHMANN'S® Active Dry Yeast**
½ **cup warm milk (100° to 110°F)**
½ **cup (1 stick) butter or margarine, softened**
2 **tablespoons sugar**
1 **teaspoon salt**
4 **cups all-purpose flour**
2 **eggs**
1 **egg, lightly beaten with 1 tablespoon water**
¼ **cup sugar**
1 **cup chopped almonds**

Place warm water in large warm bowl. Sprinkle in yeast; stir until dissolved. Add warm milk, butter, 2 tablespoons sugar, salt and 2 cups flour. Beat 2 minutes at medium speed of electric mixer. Add 2 eggs and ½ cup flour. Beat 2 minutes at high speed, scraping bowl occasionally. Stir in enough remaining flour to make soft dough. Knead on lightly floured surface until smooth and elastic, about 10 minutes. Place in greased bowl, turning to grease top. Cover; let rise in warm, draft-free place until doubled in size, about 1 hour.

Punch dough down; turn out onto lightly floured surface. Divide into 24 equal pieces. Shape each piece into smooth ball. Place in greased 2½-inch muffin cups. Cover; let rise in warm, draft-free place until doubled in size, about 30 minutes. Brush top with egg mixture. Sprinkle ¼ cup sugar and almonds over top. Bake at 375°F for 20 minutes or until done. Remove from pans; cool on wire racks.   *Makes 24 buns*

Tip There are several warm places to let dough rise. Place it inside a gas oven warmed by a pilot light or in an electric oven heated to 200°F for 1 minute and then turned off. Your microwave can also be used. Bring 2 cups water to a boil in the microwave, then turn off the power, set the dough inside and close the door.

Main Dishes

Southern Buttermilk Fried Chicken

- **2 cups all-purpose flour**
- **1½ teaspoons celery salt**
- **1 teaspoon dried thyme**
- **¾ teaspoon black pepper**
- **½ teaspoon dried marjoram**
- **1¾ cups buttermilk**
- **2 cups vegetable oil**
- **3 pounds chicken pieces**

1. Combine flour, celery salt, thyme, pepper and marjoram in shallow bowl. Pour buttermilk into medium bowl.

2. Heat oil in heavy deep skillet over medium heat until 340°F on deep-fry thermometer.

3. Dip chicken in buttermilk, one piece at a time; shake off excess. Coat with flour mixture; shake off excess. Dip again in buttermilk and coat once more with flour mixture. Fry chicken in batches, skin side down, 10 to 12 minutes or until browned. Turn and fry 12 to 14 minutes or until cooked through (170°F for breast meat; 180°F for dark meat). Allow temperature of oil to return to 350°F between batches. Drain chicken on paper towels.   *Makes 4 servings*

Note: Carefully monitor the temperature of the vegetable oil during cooking. It should not drop below 325°F or go higher than 350°F. The chicken can also be cooked in a deep fryer following the manufacturer's directions. Never leave hot oil unattended.

Old-Fashioned Meat Loaf

　1 teaspoon olive oil
　1 cup finely chopped onion
　4 cloves garlic, minced
1½ pounds ground beef
　¾ cup old-fashioned oats
　2 egg whites
　1 cup chili sauce, divided
　½ teaspoon black pepper
　¼ teaspoon salt (optional)
　1 tablespoon Dijon mustard

1. Preheat oven to 375°F. Heat oil in large nonstick skillet over medium heat. Add onion; cook and stir 5 minutes. Add garlic; cook 1 minute. Remove from heat; transfer to large bowl. Let cool 5 minutes.

2. Add beef, oats, egg whites, ½ cup chili sauce, pepper and salt, if desired; mix well. Pack into 9×5-inch loaf pan. Combine remaining ½ cup chili sauce and mustard in small bowl; spoon evenly over top of meat loaf.

3. Bake 45 to 50 minutes or until internal temperature reaches 160°F. Let stand 5 minutes. Pour off any juices from pan. Cut into slices to serve.

Makes 6 servings

Tuscan Roast Pork Tenderloin

1⅓ cups FRENCH'S® French Fried Onions
　1 teaspoon crushed rosemary leaves
　½ teaspoon garlic powder
　¼ teaspoon ground black pepper
　1 to 1½ pounds pork tenderloin
　2 tablespoons FRENCH'S® Spicy Brown Mustard

1. Mix French Fried Onions, rosemary, garlic powder and pepper in plastic bag. Crush with hands or rolling pin.

2. Brush pork with mustard. Coat in seasoned onion crumbs; press firmly to adhere.

3. Bake pork on a foil-lined baking sheet at 400°F for 30 minutes or until 155°F internal temperature. Let rest 10 minutes before slicing.

Makes 6 servings

Tip: Use this savory coating for pork chops or chicken breasts.

Prep Time: 10 minutes
Cook Time: 30 minutes

Orange and Maple Glazed Roast Turkey

1 small turkey (10 pounds), thawed if frozen
½ cup water
  Vegetable oil
¼ cup (½ stick) butter
½ cup orange juice
2 tablespoons maple syrup
½ teaspoon chili powder
¼ teaspoon salt
⅛ teaspoon black pepper
1 cup chicken broth, divided
1 to 2 teaspoons all-purpose flour

1. Preheat oven to 325°F. Remove any packets from turkey cavity. Tuck ends of turkey drumsticks into cavity; tuck tips of wings under turkey.

2. Place turkey on rack in shallow roasting pan; add water to pan. Lightly brush turkey with oil; cover loosely with heavy-duty foil. Roast turkey 1 hour, 15 minutes. Remove foil and roast, uncovered, 1 hour.

3. Melt butter in small saucepan over medium heat. Stir in orange juice, maple syrup, chili powder, salt and pepper; bring to a simmer. Remove turkey from oven; generously brush or pour glaze over turkey.

4. Roast 30 to 45 minutes or until turkey is golden brown and meat thermometer inserted into thickest part of thigh registers 165°F. Remove turkey from oven; cover loosely with foil. Set aside 15 to 20 minutes.

5. Remove turkey to serving platter. Skim fat from roasting pan. Place pan on stovetop; heat over medium heat. Pour in ¾ cup chicken broth, scraping up browned bits on bottom of pan with wooden spoon. Stir flour and remaining ¼ cup chicken broth in small cup until smooth. Pour into roasting pan. Cook over low heat, stirring constantly, until slightly thickened. If gravy is too thick, add additional broth or water. Slice turkey and serve with gravy.   *Makes 8 servings*

Oven Barbecue Chicken

  1 cup barbecue sauce
¼ cup honey
  2 tablespoons soy sauce
  2 teaspoons grated fresh ginger
½ teaspoon dry mustard
  1 chicken, cut up (about 3½ pounds)

1. Preheat oven to 350°F. Combine barbecue sauce, honey, soy sauce, ginger and mustard in small bowl; mix well.

2. Place chicken in lightly greased baking dish. Brush evenly with sauce mixture. Bake 45 minutes or until cooked through (165°F), brushing occasionally with sauce.

Makes 4 to 6 servings

Prep Time: 5 minutes
Cook Time: 45 minutes

Savory Garlic Steak with Charred Tomato Salsa

½ cup LAWRY'S® Italian Garlic Steak Marinade With
     Roasted Garlic & Olive Oil
  1 pound boneless flank steak
1½ teaspoons LAWRY'S® Garlic Salt
  1 medium onion, cut into ½-inch rings
1½ pounds whole vine ripened tomatoes
  2 tablespoons chopped fresh cilantro
  2 tablespoons lime juice
  1 chipotle chili in adobo sauce, finely chopped

1. In large resealable plastic bag, pour LAWRY'S® Italian Garlic Steak Marinade With Roasted Garlic & Olive Oil over steak; turn to coat. Close bag and marinate in refrigerator 30 minutes.

2. Remove steak from Marinade, discarding Marinade. Grill or broil steak, turning once, 8 minutes or until desired doneness. Remove and keep warm.

3. Meanwhile, evenly sprinkle ½ teaspoon LAWRY'S® Garlic Salt on onion. Grill or broil onion and tomatoes, turning once, 10 minutes or until browned. Chop tomatoes and onion; stir in remaining ingredients. Serve with grilled steak.

Makes 4 servings

Prep Time: 15 minutes
Marinate Time: 30 minutes
Cook Time: 10 minutes

Porcupine Meatballs

1 tablespoon butter or margarine
1 small onion, chopped
1 pound lean ground beef *
1 cup MINUTE® White Rice, uncooked
1 egg, lightly beaten
1 small packet meatloaf seasoning
¼ cup water
1 jar (15½ ounces or larger) spaghetti sauce

Or substitute ground turkey.

Melt butter in small skillet over medium-high heat. Add onion; cook and stir until tender. Place onion, meat, rice, egg and seasoning in large bowl. Add water; mix until well blended. Shape into medium-sized meatballs. Pour spaghetti sauce into skillet. Bring to a boil. Add meatballs; return to a boil. Reduce heat to low; cover. Simmer 15 minutes or until meatballs are cooked through.   *Makes 4 servings*

Tip To quickly shape uniform meatballs, place meat mixture on cutting board and pat evenly into a large square, one-inch thick. With a sharp knife, cut meat into 1-inch squares; shape each square into a ball.

Nutty Oven-Fried Chicken Drumsticks

12 chicken drumsticks (about 3 pounds)
1 egg, beaten
1 cup cornflake crumbs
⅓ cup finely chopped pecans
1 tablespoon sugar
1½ teaspoons salt
½ teaspoon onion powder
½ teaspoon black pepper
¼ cup (½ stick) butter or margarine, melted

1. Preheat oven to 400°F. Toss chicken with egg to coat.

2. Combine cornflake crumbs, pecans, sugar, salt, onion powder and pepper in large resealable food storage bag. Add chicken, two pieces at a time; shake to coat.

3. Place chicken on foil-lined baking sheet; drizzle with melted butter. Bake 40 to 45 minutes or until cooked through.

Makes 4 to 6 servings

Sicilian Steak Pinwheels

¾ pound mild or hot Italian sausage, casing removed
1¾ cups fresh bread crumbs
¾ cup grated Parmesan cheese
2 eggs
3 tablespoons minced parsley, plus additional for garnish
1½ to 2 pounds round steak
1 cup frozen peas
Kitchen string, cut into 15-inch lengths
1 cup pasta sauce
1 cup beef broth

Slow Cooker Directions

1. Coat 6-quart slow cooker with nonstick cooking spray. Mix sausage, bread crumbs, cheese, eggs and 3 tablespoons parsley in large bowl until well blended; set aside.

2. Place round steak between 2 large sheets of plastic wrap. Pound steak using tenderizer mallet or back of skillet until meat is about ⅜ inch thick. Remove top layer of plastic wrap. Spread sausage mixture over steak. Press frozen peas into sausage mixture. Lift edge of plastic wrap at short end to begin rolling steak. Roll up completely. Tie at 2-inch intervals with kitchen string. Transfer to slow cooker.

3. Combine pasta sauce and broth in medium bowl. Pour over meat. Cover; cook on LOW 6 hours or until meat is tender and sausage is cooked through.

4. Transfer steak to serving platter. Let stand 20 minutes before removing string and slicing. Meanwhile, skim and discard excess fat from sauce. Serve steak slices with sauce.

Makes 4 to 6 servings

Prep Time: 20 to 25 minutes
Cook Time: 6 hours

Enchilada Slow-Roasted Baby Back Ribs

  1 packet (1.25 ounces) ORTEGA® Fajita Seasoning Mix
  4 tablespoons packed brown sugar
  4 slabs baby back ribs (about 10 pounds)
  ½ cup Dijon mustard
  2 jars (8 ounces each) ORTEGA® Enchilada Sauce

Preheat oven to 250°F. Combine seasoning mix and brown sugar in small bowl. Place large piece of aluminum foil on counter. On foil, brush both sides of ribs with mustard; sprinkle both sides with seasoning mixture.

Adjust one oven rack to low position. Remove remaining oven rack; arrange ribs on rack. Slide rack with ribs into upper-middle position in oven. Place foil-lined baking sheet on lower rack to collect drippings from ribs.

Roast ribs 1½ to 2 hours or until tender. Remove ribs from oven. Turn on broiler.

Brush enchilada sauce onto both sides of ribs. Transfer ribs to foil-lined baking sheet, meat side down. Broil 5 to 6 minutes or until sauce begins to bubble. Let stand 5 minutes before slicing into individual servings.

Makes 6 to 8 servings

Prep Time: 15 minutes
Start to Finish: 2 hours

Tip You can also grill these ribs. Follow the same procedures, keeping the grill temperature at about 250°F and grill with the cover on.

Cheese-Stuffed Meat Loaf

1½ pounds ground beef
1 jar (1 pound 10 ounces) RAGÚ® Chunky Pasta Sauce, divided
1 egg, lightly beaten
¼ cup plain dry bread crumbs
2 cups (about 8 ounces) shredded mozzarella cheese
1 tablespoon finely chopped fresh parsley

1. Preheat oven to 350°F. In large bowl, combine ground beef, ⅓ cup Pasta Sauce, egg and bread crumbs. Season, if desired, with salt and ground black pepper. In 13×9-inch baking or roasting pan, shape meat mixture into 12×8-inch rectangle.

2. Sprinkle 1½ cups cheese and parsley down center of meat loaf leaving ¾-inch border. Roll, starting at long end, jelly-roll style. Press ends together to seal.

3. Bake uncovered 45 minutes. Pour remaining Pasta Sauce over meat loaf and sprinkle with remaining ½ cup cheese. Bake an additional 15 minutes or until sauce is heated through and cheese is melted. Let stand 5 minutes before serving.

Makes 6 servings

Prep Time: 20 minutes
Cook Time: 1 hour

Turkey Wienerschnitzel

   1 cup sour cream
   ⅔ cup plus 2 tablespoons all-purpose flour, divided
   2 teaspoons sweet or hot paprika
1½ teaspoons salt, divided
1½ pounds boneless, skinless turkey breast pieces
   1 egg
   ½ cup plus 3 tablespoons water, divided
   ½ teaspoon black pepper
   3 tablespoons canola or vegetable oil

1. Preheat oven to 200°F. Blend sour cream, 2 tablespoons flour, paprika and ½ teaspoon salt in small bowl; set aside. Pound turkey breast between sheets of waxed paper to ⅛-inch thickness.

2. Beat egg and 3 tablespoons water in large shallow dish. Combine remaining ⅔ cup flour, 1 teaspoon salt and pepper in large resealable food storage bag. Place turkey pieces in egg mixture; turn to coat. Transfer to bag with flour mixture; shake to coat.

3. Heat oil in large skillet over medium-high heat. Shake excess flour from turkey; add to skillet. Cook until golden brown on both sides, about 4 minutes per side. Remove to ovenproof platter; place in oven to keep warm.

4. Add remaining ½ cup water to skillet; stir over medium heat, scraping up any brown bits from bottom of pan. Whisk in sour cream mixture; cook, stirring constantly, about 1 minute or until sauce is bubbly and no lumps remain. (If the sauce is too thick, add water, 1 tablespoon at a time.) Spoon sauce over turkey; serve.   *Makes 4 servings*

Pork Chops with Cranberry-Jalapeño Relish

   ½ cup plus 2 tablespoons LAWRY'S® Hawaiian Marinade With Tropical
         Fruit Juices
   4 bone-in pork chops, about 1-inch thick (about 2 pounds)
   2 medium red, orange, yellow and/or green bell peppers, diced
   2 jalapeño peppers, seeded and diced*
   1 medium cucumber, seeded and diced
   ½ large red onion, diced
   ½ cup chopped dried cranberries or apricots
   ¼ teaspoon LAWRY'S® Garlic Salt

Jalapeño peppers can sting and irritate the skin, so wear rubber gloves when handling peppers and do not touch eyes.

continued on page 152

Pork Chops with Cranberry-Jalapeño Relish, continued

1. In large resealable plastic bag, pour ½ cup LAWRY'S® Hawaiian Marinade With Tropical Fruit Juices over chops; turn to coat. Close bag and marinate in refrigerator 30 minutes.

2. In medium bowl, combine 2 tablespoons Marinade with remaining ingredients.

3. Remove chops from Marinade, discarding Marinade. Grill chops, turning once, 15 minutes or until chops are done. To serve, arrange chops on serving platter and top with relish.

Variation: Also terrific with LAWRY'S® Caribbean Jerk Marinade With Papaya Juice.

Makes 4 servings

Prep Time: 25 minutes
Marinate Time: 30 minutes
Cook Time: 15 minutes

Steak Diane with Cremini Mushrooms

2 beef tenderloin steaks (4 ounces each), cut ¾ inch thick
¼ teaspoon black pepper
⅓ cup sliced shallots or chopped onion
4 ounces cremini mushrooms, sliced *or* 1 (4-ounce) package sliced, mixed, exotic mushrooms
1½ tablespoons Worcestershire sauce
1 tablespoon Dijon mustard

1. Lightly coat large nonstick skillet with cooking spray; heat over medium-high heat. Add steaks; sprinkle with pepper. Sear steaks 3 minutes per side for medium-rare or to desired doneness. Transfer steaks to plate; set aside.

2. Spray same skillet with cooking spray; place over medium heat. Add shallots; cook 2 minutes. Add mushrooms; cook 3 minutes, stirring frequently. Add Worcestershire sauce and mustard; cook 1 minute, stirring frequently.

3. Return steaks and any accumulated juices to skillet; heat through, turning once. Transfer steaks to serving plates; top with mushroom mixture.

Makes 2 servings

Southwestern Chicken and Black Bean Skillet

1 teaspoon ground cumin
1 teaspoon ground chili powder
½ teaspoon salt
4 boneless skinless chicken breasts
2 teaspoons canola or vegetable oil
1 cup chopped yellow onion
1 red bell pepper, chopped
1 can (about 15 ounces) black beans, rinsed and drained
½ cup chunky salsa
¼ cup chopped fresh cilantro or thinly sliced green onion (optional)

1. Sprinkle cumin, chili powder and salt over chicken. Heat oil in large nonstick skillet over medium-high heat. Add chicken; cook 2 minutes per side. Transfer chicken to plate; set aside.

2. Add onion to skillet; cook 1 minute, stirring occasionally. Add bell pepper; cook over medium heat 5 minutes, stirring occasionally. Add beans and salsa; mix well. Place chicken over bean mixture. Cover; cook 6 to 7 minutes or until chicken is cooked through. Top with cilantro. *Makes 4 servings*

Tip

Salsa is the Spanish word for sauce. In America, it is a generic term that refers to a large, diverse group of chunky, usually highly seasoned mixtures. Salsas can be made at home from fresh ingredients or purchased. They can be based on fruits (such as papaya, mango and peaches), corn, black beans and/or vegetables.

Spicy Citrus Pork with Pineapple Salsa

1½ teaspoons ground cumin
¼ teaspoon salt
½ teaspoon coarsely ground black pepper
1½ pounds center-cut pork loin, rinsed and patted dry
1 tablespoon vegetable oil
2 cans (8 ounces each) pineapple tidbits* in juice, drained, ¼ cup juice reserved, divided
2 tablespoons lemon juice, divided
1 teaspoon grated lemon peel
½ cup finely chopped orange or red bell pepper
2 tablespoons finely chopped red onion
1 tablespoon chopped fresh cilantro or mint
½ teaspoon grated fresh ginger (optional)
⅛ teaspoon red pepper flakes (optional)

*If tidbits are unavailable, purchase pineapple chunks and coarsely chop.

Slow Cooker Directions

1. Coat 2½-quart slow cooker with nonstick cooking spray. Combine cumin, salt and black pepper in small bowl. Rub evenly onto pork. Heat oil in medium skillet over medium-high heat. Sear pork 1 to 2 minutes per side. Transfer to slow cooker.

2. Spoon 2 tablespoons reserved pineapple juice and 1 tablespoon lemon juice over pork. Cover; cook on LOW 2 to 2 hours, 15 minutes or on HIGH 1 hour, 10 minutes or until meat thermometer registers 160°F and pork is barely pink in center. (Do not overcook.)

3. Meanwhile, combine pineapple, remaining 2 tablespoons pineapple juice, remaining 1 tablespoon lemon juice, lemon peel, bell pepper, onion, cilantro, ginger, if desired, and pepper flakes, if desired, in medium bowl. Toss gently and blend well; set aside.

4. Transfer pork to serving platter. Let stand 10 minutes before slicing. To serve, pour sauce evenly over slices. Serve with salsa. *Makes 6 servings*

Prep Time: 15 minutes
Cook Time: 2 to 2 hours, 15 minutes (LOW) or 1 hour, 10 minutes (HIGH)

On the Side

Twice-Baked Potatoes with Sun-Dried Tomatoes

  4 large baking potatoes
    Vegetable oil
  1 container (16 ounces) sour cream
  2 cups (8 ounces) shredded Cheddar cheese, divided
  ⅓ cup sun-dried tomatoes packed in oil, drained and chopped
  4 tablespoons finely chopped green onions, divided
  2 tablespoons butter, softened
  1 teaspoon salt
  ½ teaspoon black pepper

1. Preheat oven to 350°F. Scrub potatoes and pat dry with paper towels. Rub potatoes with vegetable oil; bake 1 hour. Cool 30 minutes.

2. Cut each potato in half lengthwise. Scrape potato pulp into large bowl, leaving ½-inch thick shells. Add sour cream, 1½ cups cheese, sun-dried tomatoes, 3 tablespoons green onions, butter, salt and pepper; mix gently. Fill potato shells.

3. Bake 15 to 20 minutes or until heated through. Top with remaining ½ cup cheese; bake 5 minutes or until cheese is melted. Sprinkle with remaining green onions.

Makes 8 servings

Salsa-Buttered Corn on the Cob

6 ears fresh corn, shucked
4 tablespoons butter, softened
¼ cup ORTEGA® Salsa
2 tablespoons ORTEGA® Taco Seasoning Mix, or to taste

Bring large pot of water to a boil. Add corn; cook 5 to 10 minutes.

Combine butter and salsa in small bowl; mix well. Place seasoning mix in another small bowl. Spread salsa butter onto cooked corn and sprinkle on seasoning mix, to taste. *Makes 6 servings*

Variation: For a different side dish, cut the corn off the cob and heat in a skillet with the salsa butter and taco seasoning mix.

Prep Time: 5 minutes
Start to Finish: 20 minutes

Spinach Artichoke Gratin

Nonstick cooking spray
2 cups cottage cheese
2 eggs
4½ tablespoons grated Parmesan cheese, divided
1 tablespoon lemon juice
⅛ teaspoon black pepper
⅛ teaspoon ground nutmeg
2 packages (10 ounces each) frozen chopped spinach, thawed
⅓ cup thinly sliced green onions
1 package (10 ounces) frozen artichoke hearts, thawed and halved

1. Preheat oven to 375°F. Coat 1½-quart baking dish with cooking spray.

2. Process cottage cheese, eggs, 3 tablespoons cheese, lemon juice, pepper and nutmeg in food processor until smooth.

3. Squeeze moisture from spinach. Combine spinach, cottage cheese mixture and green onions in large bowl. Spread half of mixture in baking dish.

4. Pat artichoke halves dry with paper towels. Place in single layer over spinach mixture. Sprinkle with remaining cheese. Cover with remaining spinach mixture. Bake, covered, 25 minutes. *Makes 6 servings*

Green Bean Casserole

1 can (10¾ ounces) Campbell's® Condensed Cream of Mushroom Soup
    (Regular *or* 98% Fat Free)
½ cup milk
1 teaspoon soy sauce
    Dash ground black pepper
2 packages (10 ounces *each*) frozen cut green beans, cooked and drained
1 can (2.8 ounces) French fried onions (1⅓ cups)

1. Stir the soup, milk, soy sauce, black pepper, green beans and ⅔ cup onions in a
1½-quart casserole.

2. Bake at 350°F. for 25 minutes or until hot. Stir the green bean mixture.

3. Sprinkle the remaining onions over the green bean mixture. Bake for 5 minutes
more or until onions are golden brown.   *Makes 5 servings*

Easy Substitution: You can also make this classic side dish with fresh or canned green
beans. You will need either 1½ pounds fresh green beans, cut into 1-inch pieces,
cooked and drained or 2 cans (about 16 ounces each) cut green beans, drained for the
frozen green beans.

Start to Finish Time: 40 minutes
Prepping: 10 minutes
Baking: 30 minutes

Thyme-Scented Roasted Sweet Potatoes and Onions

2 large, unpeeled sweet potatoes (about 1¼ pounds)
2 tablespoons canola oil
1 medium sweet or yellow onion, cut into chunks
1 teaspoon dried thyme
½ teaspoon salt
½ teaspoon smoked paprika
⅛ teaspoon ground red pepper (optional)

1. Preheat oven to 425°F. Coat 15×10-inch jelly-roll pan with nonstick cooking spray.

2. Cut sweet potatoes into 1-inch chunks; place in large bowl. Add oil; toss well. Add
onion, thyme, salt, paprika and red pepper, if desired; toss well.

3. Spread vegetables in single layer on prepared pan. Bake 20 to 25 minutes or until
very tender, stirring after 10 minutes. Let stand 5 minutes before serving.

Makes 10 servings

Chunky Ranch Potatoes

3 pounds medium red potatoes, unpeeled and quartered
1 cup water
½ cup prepared ranch dressing
½ cup grated Parmesan or Cheddar cheese (optional)
¼ cup minced chives

Slow Cooker Directions

1. Place potatoes in 4-quart slow cooker. Add water. Cover; cook on LOW 7 to 9 hours or on HIGH 4 to 6 hours or until potatoes are tender.

2. Stir in ranch dressing, cheese, if desired, and chives. Use spoon to break up potatoes into chunks. Serve hot or cold. *Makes 8 servings*

Prep Time: 10 minutes
Cook Time: 7 to 9 hours (LOW) or 4 to 6 hours (HIGH)

Glazed Parsnips and Carrots

1 pound parsnips (2 very large or 3 medium)
8 ounces baby carrots
1 tablespoon canola oil
  Salt and black pepper
¼ cup orange juice
1 tablespoon unsalted butter or margarine
1 tablespoon honey
⅛ teaspoon ground ginger

1. Preheat oven to 425°F. Peel parsnips; cut into wedges the same size as baby carrots.

2. Spread vegetables in shallow roasting pan. Drizzle with oil and sprinkle with salt and pepper; toss to coat. Bake 30 to 35 minutes or until fork-tender.

3. Combine orange juice, butter, honey and ginger in large skillet. Add roasted vegetables; cook and stir over high heat 1 to 2 minutes, stirring frequently, until sauce thickens and coats vegetables. Season with additional salt and pepper, if desired.
Makes 6 servings

Fennel Braised with Tomato

2 bulbs fennel
1 tablespoon extra-virgin olive oil
1 small onion, sliced
1 clove garlic, sliced
4 medium tomatoes, chopped
⅔ cup plus 3 tablespoons vegetable broth or water
1 tablespoon chopped fresh marjoram *or* 1 teaspoon dried marjoram
¼ teaspoon salt
¼ teaspoon black pepper

1. Trim stems and bottoms from fennel bulbs, reserving green leafy tops for garnish. Cut each bulb lengthwise into 4 wedges.

2. Heat oil in large skillet over medium heat. Cook fennel, onion and garlic, stirring occasionally, until onion is soft and translucent, about 5 minutes.

3. Add tomatoes, broth and marjoram. Season with salt and pepper. Cover; simmer gently until fennel is tender, about 20 minutes. Garnish with fennel leaves.

Makes 6 servings

Ham Seasoned Peas

1 teaspoon olive oil
¼ pound cooked ham, chopped
¼ cup chopped onion
2 cups (about 9 ounces) frozen peas
¼ cup chicken broth
⅛ to ¼ teaspoon dried oregano
⅛ teaspoon black pepper (optional)

1. Heat oil in medium saucepan. Add ham and onion; cook until onion is tender.

2. Stir in peas, broth, oregano and pepper, if desired. Bring to a boil. Reduce heat; simmer, covered, 4 to 5 minutes or until peas are tender.

Makes 4 servings

Prep Time: 5 minutes
Cook Time: 10 minutes

Creamy Golden Mushroom Mashed Potatoes

  6 medium baking potatoes, cut into 1-inch pieces (about 6 cups)
  1 small onion, cut into wedges
     Water
  1 can (10¾ ounces) Campbell's® Condensed Golden Mushroom Soup
  ¾ cup milk
  ¼ cup heavy cream
  4 tablespoons butter

1. Put the potatoes and onion in a 4-quart saucepot with enough water to cover them. Heat the potatoes over medium-high heat to a boil. Reduce the heat to low. Cover and cook the potatoes for 20 minutes or until they're fork-tender. Drain the potatoes and onion well in a colander.

2. Put the potatoes and onion in a 3-quart bowl and beat with an electric mixer at medium speed until almost smooth.

3. Put the soup, milk, cream and butter in a 4-cup microwavable measuring cup. Microwave on HIGH for 2½ minutes or until hot. Slowly pour the hot soup mixture into the potatoes, beating with an electric mixer at medium speed until the potatoes are smooth. Season to taste.   *Makes 6 servings*

Start to Finish Time: 50 minutes
Prep Time: 20 minutes
Cook Time: 30 minutes

Spanish Stewed Tomatoes

  2 tablespoons olive oil
  ½ teaspoon POLANER® Chopped Garlic
  1 can (15 ounces) diced tomatoes
  ½ cup water
  1 packet (1.25 ounces) ORTEGA® Taco Seasoning Mix
  2 cups frozen green beans
  2 tablespoons ORTEGA® Diced Green Chiles

Heat oil in medium skillet over medium heat until hot. Add garlic. Cook and stir until golden brown. Stir in tomatoes, water and seasoning mix. Simmer 3 minutes. Add beans and chiles; simmer 4 minutes longer or until beans are heated through.

Makes 6 servings

Variation: Replace the green beans with corn or lima beans.

Prep Time: 5 minutes
Start to Finish: 15 minutes

Grilled Ratatouille

1¼ cups LAWRY'S® Herb & Garlic Marinade With Lemon Juice
3 medium tomatoes, halved
1 medium zucchini, halved lengthwise
1 medium yellow squash, halved lengthwise
1 medium eggplant (about 1½ pounds), cut into ¼-inch thick slices
1 large red onion, cut into ½-inch thick slices
4 ounces Parmigiano-Reggiano cheese, shaved

1. In 13×9-inch glass baking dish, combine LAWRY'S® Herb & Garlic Marinade With Lemon Juice with vegetables. Cover and marinate 30 minutes.

2. Remove vegetables from Marinade, reserving Marinade. Grill vegetables, turning occasionally and brushing frequently with reserved Marinade, 12 minutes or until tender; coarsely chop. Top with cheese. Serve, if desired, with hot cooked rice.

Makes 7 cups

Variation: Also terrific with LAWRY'S® Italian Garlic Steak Marinade With Roasted Garlic & Olive Oil.

Prep Time: 10 minutes
Marinate Time: 30 minutes
Cook Time: 12 minutes

Garlic and Chipotle Cheddar Mashed Potatoes

5 pounds russet potatoes, peeled and cut into 1-inch pieces
36 cloves garlic, roasted*
1¾ cups (7 ounces) SARGENTO® Bistro® Blends Shredded Chipotle Cheddar Cheese
4 ounces cream cheese, room temperature
¼ cup (½ stick) unsalted butter, room temperature

To roast garlic, slice top point off each of three bulbs of garlic. Drizzle with ⅓ cup olive oil. Roast at 400°F for 45 minutes. Cool. Reserve garlic oil for another use. Squeeze garlic cloves out of skins.

Cook potatoes in large pot of boiling salted water until tender, about 25 minutes. Drain. Add garlic, cheeses and butter. Mash mixture until smooth. Season to taste with salt and pepper.

Makes 8 servings

Creamy Spinach-Stuffed Portobellos

4 large portobello mushrooms
1 tablespoon vegetable oil
1 medium onion, chopped (about ½ cup)
1 medium tomato, chopped (about 1 cup)
1 bag (6 ounces) baby spinach leaves, washed
1 can (10¾ ounces) Campbell's® Condensed Cream of Celery Soup
  (Regular *or* 98% Fat Free)
2 tablespoons grated Parmesan cheese
1 tablespoon dry bread crumbs, toasted

1. Remove the stems from the mushrooms. Set the caps topside down in a 13×9×2-inch baking pan.

2. Heat the oil in a 10-inch nonstick skillet over medium heat. Add the onion and cook until the onion is tender-crisp. Add the tomatoes and spinach and cook just until the spinach is wilted. Stir in the soup and heat through.

3. Spoon the filling into the mushroom caps.

4. Bake at 425°F. for 15 minutes or until mushrooms are hot.

5. Mix the cheese with bread crumbs in a small cup. Sprinkle over the mushrooms.

6. Heat the broiler. Broil the mushrooms with the top of the mushrooms 4 inches from the heat for about 5 minutes or until topping is golden.   *Makes 4 servings*

Start to Finish Time: 30 minutes
Prepping: 10 minutes
Baking/Broiling Time: 20 minutes

Almond and Vanilla Green Beans

1½ pounds fresh green beans, trimmed
 ⅓ cup sliced almonds
 ¼ cup (½ stick) butter
2½ teaspoons WATKINS® Vanilla Extract
  Salt and WATKINS® Black Pepper, to taste

Cook beans until crisp-tender; drain well and keep warm. Cook and stir almonds in butter until golden brown. Remove from heat; stir in vanilla, salt and pepper. Pour over beans; serve hot.   *Makes 9 servings*

Chutney Glazed Carrots

  2 cups cut peeled carrots (1½-inch pieces)
  3 tablespoons cranberry or mango chutney
  1 tablespoon Dijon mustard
  2 teaspoons butter
  2 tablespoons chopped pecans, toasted*

*To toast pecans, spread in single layer on ungreased baking sheet. Bake in preheated 350°F oven 5 to 7 minutes or until fragrant, stirring occasionally.

1. Place carrots in medium saucepan; cover with water. Bring to a boil over high heat. Reduce heat; simmer 6 to 8 minutes or until carrots are tender.

2. Drain carrots; return to pan. Add chutney, mustard and butter. Cook, stirring constantly, over medium heat about 2 minutes or until carrots are glazed. Top with pecans.   *Makes 4 servings*

Prep Time: 5 minutes
Cook Time: 10 minutes

Candied Sweet Potatoes

  MAZOLA PURE® Cooking Spray
  1 can (29 ounces) cut sweet potatoes, drained
  3 tablespoons butter or margarine
  ½ cup KARO® Light or Dark Corn Syrup
  3 tablespoons sugar
  ¾ teaspoon salt
  ¾ teaspoon ground cinnamon

1. Coat shallow 1½- to 2-quart baking dish with cooking spray. Place sweet potatoes in prepared dish.

2. In small saucepan over low heat melt butter. Stir in corn syrup, sugar, salt and cinnamon. Cook and stir 1 to 2 minutes or until smooth. Pour evenly over sweet potatoes; stir gently to coat.

3. Bake in 350°F oven 20 minutes or until hot and bubbly.   *Makes 4 to 6 servings*

Prep Time: 10 minutes
Cook Time: 20 minutes

Delicious Desserts

Chocolate Vanilla Swirl Cheesecake

20 OREO® Chocolate Sandwich Cookies, crushed (about 2 cups)
3 tablespoons butter, melted
4 packages (8 ounces each) PHILADELPHIA® Cream Cheese, softened
1 cup sugar
1 teaspoon vanilla
1 cup BREAKSTONE'S® or KNUDSEN® Sour Cream
4 eggs
6 squares BAKER'S® Semi-Sweet Baking Chocolate, melted, cooled

PREHEAT oven to 325°F. Line 13×9-inch baking pan with foil, with ends of foil extending over sides of pan. Mix cookie crumbs and butter; press firmly onto bottom of prepared pan. Bake 10 minutes.

BEAT cream cheese, sugar and vanilla in large bowl with electric mixer on medium speed until well blended. Add sour cream; mix well. Add eggs, 1 at a time, beating on low speed after each addition just until blended. Remove 1 cup of the batter; set aside. Stir melted chocolate into remaining batter. Pour chocolate batter over crust; top with spoonfuls of remaining plain batter. Cut through batters with knife several times for swirled effect.

BAKE 40 minutes or until center is almost set. Cool. Refrigerate at least 4 hours or overnight. Use foil handles to lift cheesecake from pan before cutting to serve. Store any leftover cheesecake in refrigerator.   *Makes 16 servings, 1 piece each*

Prep Time: 15 minutes plus refrigerating
Bake Time: 40 minutes

Tip: Jazz It Up! Garnish with chocolate curls just before serving. Use a vegetable peeler to shave the side of an additional square of BAKER'S® Semi-Sweet Baking Chocolate and a square of BAKER'S® Premium White Baking Chocolate until desired amount of curls are obtained. Wrap remaining chocolate and store at room temperature for another use.

Chocolate Croissant Pudding

1½ **cups milk**
 3 **eggs**
½ **cup sugar**
¼ **cup unsweetened cocoa powder**
½ **teaspoon vanilla**
¼ **teaspoon salt**
 2 **plain croissants, cut into 1-inch pieces**
½ **cup chocolate chips**
   Whipped cream

Slow Cooker Directions

1. Beat milk, eggs, sugar, cocoa, vanilla and salt in medium bowl.

2. Grease 1-quart casserole. Layer half of croissants, chocolate chips and half of egg mixture in casserole. Repeat layers with remaining croissants and egg mixture.

3. Add rack to 5-quart slow cooker; pour in 1 cup water. Place casserole on rack. Cover; cook on LOW 3 to 4 hours. Remove pudding from slow cooker. Serve with whipped cream.   *Makes 6 servings*

Carrot Cake with Black Walnut Frosting

 1 **cup granulated sugar**
 3 **eggs**
⅔ **cup WATKINS® Original Grapeseed Oil**
 1 **teaspoon WATKINS® Vanilla**
1½ **cups all-purpose flour**
 2 **teaspoons WATKINS® Ground Cinnamon**
½ **teaspoon WATKINS® Ground Cloves**
½ **teaspoon WATKINS® Nutmeg**
½ **teaspoon WATKINS® Allspice**
1½ **teaspoons baking soda**
 1 **teaspoon WATKINS® Baking Powder**
½ **teaspoon salt**
 2 **cups finely grated carrots**
 1 **cup walnuts, chopped**
 1 **package (8 ounces) cream cheese**
⅓ **cup butter, at room temperature**
½ **teaspoon WATKINS® Vanilla Nut Extract**
½ **teaspoon WATKINS® Butter Pecan or Vanilla Nut Extract**
2½ **cups powdered sugar**

continued on page 178

Carrot Cake with Black Walnut Frosting, continued

Preheat oven to 350°F. Spray two 9×2-inch round cake pans with WATKINS® Cooking Spray; dust with flour. Combine granulated sugar, eggs and oil in large bowl; beat for 1 minute. Stir in vanilla. Add flour, spices, baking soda, baking powder and salt; beat about 1 minute. Fold in carrots and walnuts. Pour into prepared pans. Bake for 30 minutes or until toothpick inserted into center comes out clean.

Beat cream cheese, butter and extracts in medium bowl until smooth. Add powdered sugar, ½ cup at a time; beat until frosting is of spreading consistency. Fill and frost cake with frosting.   *Makes 12 servings*

Variations: Add golden raisins or pineapple to batter, if desired. Or substitute 2 cups shredded zucchini for the shredded carrots.

Cherry Crisp

   1 **(21-ounce) can cherry pie filling**
½ **teaspoon almond extract**
½ **cup all-purpose flour**
½ **cup firmly packed brown sugar**
   1 **teaspoon ground cinnamon**
   3 **tablespoons butter or margarine, softened**
½ **cup chopped walnuts**
¼ **cup flaked coconut**
      Ice cream or whipped cream (optional)

Pour cherry pie filling into ungreased 8×8×2-inch baking pan. Stir in almond extract.

Place flour, brown sugar and cinnamon in medium mixing bowl; mix well. Add butter; stir with fork until mixture is crumbly. Stir in walnuts and coconut. Sprinkle mixture over cherry pie filling.

Bake in preheated 350°F oven 25 minutes or until golden brown on top and filling is bubbly. Serve warm or at room temperature. If desired, top with ice cream or whipped cream.   *Makes 6 servings*

Note: This recipe can be doubled. Bake in two 8×8×2-inch baking pans or one 13×9×2-inch pan.

Favorite recipe from **Cherry Marketing Institute**

HERSHEY'S Brownies with Peanut Butter Frosting

½ **cup (1 stick) butter or margarine**
4 **sections (½ ounce each) HERSHEY®S Unsweetened Chocolate Premium Baking Bar, broken into pieces**
1 **cup sugar**
2 **eggs**
1 **teaspoon vanilla extract**
½ **cup all-purpose flour**
¼ **teaspoon baking powder**
¼ **teaspoon salt**
½ **cup chopped nuts**
   Peanut Butter Frosting (optional)

1. Heat oven to 350°F. Grease 8-inch square baking pan.

2. Melt butter and chocolate in medium saucepan over low heat. Remove from heat; stir in sugar. Beat in eggs and vanilla with wooden spoon. Stir together flour, baking powder and salt. Add to chocolate mixture, blending well. Stir in nuts. Pour batter into prepared pan.

3. Bake 30 to 35 minutes or until brownies begin to pull away from sides of pan. Cool completely in pan on wire rack. Frost with Peanut Butter Frosting, if desired. Cut into squares.   *Makes about 16 brownies*

Peanut Butter Frosting

1 **cup powdered sugar**
¼ **cup REESE'S® Creamy Peanut Butter**
2 **tablespoons milk**
½ **teaspoon vanilla extract**

Combine all ingredients in small bowl; beat until smooth. If necessary add additional milk, ½ teaspoon at a time, until of desired consistency.   *Makes about ¾ cup frosting*

New York-Style Sour Cream-Topped Cheesecake

1½ **cups HONEY MAID® Graham Cracker Crumbs**
 ¼ **cup (½ stick) butter, melted**
1¼ **cups sugar, divided**
  4 **packages (8 ounces each) PHILADELPHIA® Cream Cheese, softened**
  2 **teaspoons vanilla, divided**
  1 **container (16 ounces) BREAKSTONE'S® or KNUDSEN® Sour Cream, divided**
  4 **eggs**

PREHEAT oven to 325°F. Line 13×9-inch baking pan with foil, with ends of foil extending over sides of pan. Mix crumbs, butter and 2 tablespoons of the sugar; press firmly onto bottom of prepared pan.

BEAT cream cheese, 1 cup of the remaining sugar and 1 teaspoon of the vanilla in large bowl with electric mixer on medium speed until well blended. Add 1 cup of the sour cream; mix well. Add eggs, one at a time, beating on low speed after each addition just until blended. Pour over crust.

BAKE 40 minutes or until center is almost set. Mix remaining sour cream, 2 tablespoons sugar and 1 teaspoon vanilla until well blended; carefully spread over cheesecake. Bake an additional 10 minutes. Cool. Cover; refrigerate 4 hours or overnight. Lift cheesecake from pan using foil handles. Garnish as desired. Store leftover cheesecake in refrigerator.   *Makes 16 servings, 1 piece each*

Substitution: Prepare as directed, substituting 1½ cups finely crushed OREO® Chocolate Sandwich Cookies for the graham cracker crumbs.

Prep Time: 15 minutes plus refrigerating
Bake Time: 40 minutes

 To prevent cracking, do not overmix the cheesecake batter; beat just until the mixture is blended.

Chocolate Mousse Cake Roll

Chocolate Mousse Filling (page 185)
4 eggs, separated
½ cup plus ⅓ cup granulated sugar, divided
1 teaspoon vanilla extract
½ cup all-purpose flour
⅓ cup HERSHEY'S Cocoa
½ teaspoon baking powder
¼ teaspoon baking soda
⅛ teaspoon salt
⅓ cup water
Powdered sugar
HERSHEY'S Syrup

1. Prepare chocolate mousse filling. Chill 6 to 8 hours or overnight.

2. Prepare cake.* Heat oven to 375°F. Line 15½×10½×1-inch jelly-roll pan with foil; generously grease foil.

3. Beat egg whites in large bowl until soft peaks form; gradually add ½ cup granulated sugar, beating until stiff peaks form. Beat egg yolks and vanilla in medium bowl on medium speed of mixer 3 minutes. Gradually add remaining ⅓ cup granulated sugar; continue beating 2 additional minutes.

4. Stir together flour, cocoa, baking powder, baking soda and salt; add to egg yolk mixture alternately with water, beating on low speed just until batter is smooth. Gradually fold chocolate mixture into beaten egg whites until well blended. Spread batter evenly in prepared pan.

5. Bake 12 to 15 minutes or until top springs back when touched lightly in center. Immediately loosen cake from edges of pan; invert onto clean towel sprinkled with powdered sugar. Carefully peel off foil. Immediately roll cake and towel together starting from narrow end; place on wire rack to cool completely.

6. Carefully unroll cake; remove towel. Gently stir filling until of spreading consistency. Spread cake with filling; reroll cake. Refrigerate several hours. Sift powdered sugar over top just before serving. Serve drizzled with syrup and garnished as desired. Cover; refrigerate leftover cake roll. *Makes 8 to 10 servings*

Cake may be prepared up to two days in advance. Keep cake rolled tightly and covered well so that it doesn't get dry.

Chocolate Mousse Filling

¼ **cup sugar**
1 **teaspoon unflavored gelatin**
½ **cup milk**
1 **cup HERSHEY᾿S SPECIAL DARK® Chocolate Chips or**
    HERSHEY᾿S Semi-Sweet Chocolate Chips
2 **teaspoons vanilla extract**
1 **cup (½ pint) cold whipping cream**

1. Stir together sugar and gelatin in small saucepan; stir in milk. Let stand 2 minutes to soften gelatin. Cook over medium heat, stirring constantly, until mixture begins to boil.

2. Remove from heat. Immediately add chocolate chips; stir until melted. Stir in vanilla; cool to room temperature.

3. Beat whipping cream in small bowl until stiff. Gradually add chocolate mixture, folding gently just until blended. Cover; refrigerate until ready to use.

Makes about 3 cups

Flan

2 **cups sugar, divided**
½ **cup water**
1 **package (8 ounces) PHILADELPHIA® Cream Cheese, softened**
1 **can (13 ounces) evaporated milk**
4 **eggs**
1 **teaspoon vanilla**
   Dash salt

MIX 1 cup of the sugar and water in heavy saucepan. Bring to boil over medium-high heat. Boil until syrup turns deep golden brown. Remove from heat; immediately pour into 8- or 9-inch round cake pan, tilting pan to distribute syrup evenly on bottom.

BEAT cream cheese and remaining 1 cup sugar with electric mixer on medium speed until well blended. Gradually add milk, beating well after each addition. Blend in eggs, vanilla and salt. Pour into prepared pan.

PLACE pan in large baking pan; place in oven. Pour boiling water into larger pan to come about ¾ of the way up side of cake pan.

BAKE at 350°F for 1 hour and 20 minutes or until knife inserted near center comes out clean. Remove cake pan from water; cool. Cover; refrigerate several hours. To serve, run metal spatula around edge of pan. Unmold onto serving plate.

Makes 8 to 10 servings

Prep Time: 30 minutes plus refrigerating
Bake Time: 1 hour 20 minutes

Pumpkin Custard

  1 **cup solid-pack pumpkin**
  ½ **cup packed brown sugar**
  2 **eggs, beaten**
  ½ **teaspoon ground ginger**
  ½ **teaspoon grated lemon peel**
  ½ **teaspoon ground cinnamon**
  1 **can (12 ounces) evaporated milk**
    Additional ground cinnamon

Slow Cooker Directions

1. Combine pumpkin, brown sugar, eggs, ginger, lemon peel and ½ teaspoon cinnamon in large bowl. Stir in evaporated milk. Pour mixture into 1½-quart soufflé dish. Cover tightly with foil.

2. Make foil handles*. Place soufflé dish in slow cooker. Pour water into slow cooker to come about 1½ inches from top of soufflé dish. Cover; cook on LOW 4 hours.

3. Use foil handles to lift dish from slow cooker. Sprinkle with additional ground cinnamon. Serve warm.   *Makes 6 servings*

To make foil handles, tear off three 18×3-inch strips of heavy-duty foil. Crisscross the strips so they resemble the spokes of a wheel. Place the dish in the center of the strips. Pull the foil strips up and over dish. Place in the slow cooker. Leave them in while you cook so you can easily lift the dish out again when ready.

Baked Apples with Cinnamon Chip Streusel

  4 **large Michigan Golden Delicious Apples**
  ¼ **cup quick oats**
  ¼ **cup brown sugar**
  ⅓ **cup pecans**
    Pinch salt
  4 **tablespoons cold butter**
  ⅓ **cup cinnamon chips**
  1½ **cups Michigan Apple Cider**
  2 **tablespoons sugar**
  1 **tablespoon butter**
    Whipped cream or ice cream (optional)

1. Preheat oven to 350°F. Place oats, brown sugar, pecans, salt and cold butter in bowl of food processor fitted with steel blade. Pulse until mixture becomes crumbly. Transfer to medium bowl and stir in cinnamon chips. Set aside.

continued on page 188

Baked Apples with Cinnamon Chip Streusel, continued

2. Peel 1-inch strip from top of each apple. Using melon ball tool, scoop out cavity in each apple, leaving bottom intact. Fill each apple with Cinnamon Chip Streusel and place in baking dish. Pour apple cider around apples and bake 40 to 45 minutes. Remove from oven.

3. Pour apple cider from baking dish into small saucepan. Stir in sugar and simmer over medium heat until cider becomes syrupy and is reduced by half. Remove from heat and stir in butter.

4. To serve, place apple on plate and drizzle with apple cider reduction. Serve with whipped cream or ice cream, if desired.   *Makes 4 servings*

Favorite recipe from **Michigan Apple Committee**

Rustic Cranberry-Pear Galette

¼ **cup sugar, divided**
1 **tablespoon plus 1 teaspoon cornstarch**
2 **teaspoons ground cinnamon or apple pie spice**
4 **cups thinly sliced, peeled Bartlett pears**
¼ **cup dried cranberries**
1 **teaspoon vanilla**
¼ **teaspoon almond extract (optional)**
1 **refrigerated pie crust, at room temperature (half of 15-ounce package)**
1 **egg white**
1 **tablespoon water**

1. Preheat oven to 450°F. Coat pizza pan or baking sheet with nonstick cooking spray.

2. Reserve 1 teaspoon sugar. Combine remaining sugar, cornstarch and cinnamon in medium bowl; mix well. Add pears, cranberries, vanilla and almond extract, if desired; toss to coat.

3. Place crust on prepared pan. Spoon pear mixture into center of crust to within 2 inches of edge. Fold edge of crust 2 inches over pear mixture; crimp slightly.

4. Whisk egg white and water in small bowl until well blended. Brush outer edge of pie crust with egg white mixture; sprinkle with reserved 1 teaspoon sugar.

5. Bake 25 minutes or until pears are tender and crust is golden brown. If edge browns too quickly, cover with foil after 15 minutes of baking. Cool on wire rack 30 minutes.

Makes 8 servings

Apple-Pomegranate Crisp

Syrup
   1 **cup pomegranate juice**
   ¼ **cup sugar**
   1 **teaspoon cornstarch**
   1 **teaspoon ground cinnamon**

Filling
   4 **medium Granny Smith apples, thinly sliced**
   ⅓ **cup CREAM OF WHEAT® Apples 'n Cinnamon Instant Hot Cereal,**
      uncooked, divided
   1 **cup pomegranate arils**

Topping
   ½ **cup all-purpose flour**
   ¼ **cup sugar**
   1 **teaspoon ground cinnamon**
   ¼ **teaspoon salt**
   2 **tablespoons cold butter, cut into ½-inch pieces**
   2 **tablespoons apple juice**
     Frozen low-fat yogurt (optional)

1. Preheat oven to 350°F. Whisk pomegranate juice, sugar, cornstarch and cinnamon in medium saucepan until well blended. Bring to a boil over medium heat. Cook 5 minutes or until thickened, stirring constantly. Remove syrup from heat; set aside.

2. Toss apples with ¼ cup Cream of Wheat. Divide evenly into 8 (6-ounce) ramekins or ovenproof bowls. Top evenly with pomegranate arils and prepared syrup; set aside.

3. Combine flour, sugar, cinnamon, salt and remaining Cream of Wheat in medium bowl. Cut in butter with pastry blender until mixture resembles coarse crumbs. Stir in apple juice until well blended. Sprinkle topping evenly over apple mixture in each bowl.

4. Bake 25 to 30 minutes or until apples are tender and topping is golden brown. Serve warm. Top with frozen yogurt, if desired. *Makes 8 servings*

Prep Time: 20 minutes
Start to Finish Time: 45 minutes

Tip: Arils are the juicy ruby-red sacs inside fresh pomegranates that contain a tiny edible seed. To extract them from the pomegranate with no mess, section the pomegranate, and place the sections in a bowl of water. Separate the arils from the inedible membrane, and discard the skin and membrane. Lift the arils from the water and drain well before using.

Farmhouse Lemon Meringue Pie

1 frozen pie crust
4 eggs, at room temperature
3 tablespoons lemon juice
2 tablespoons butter, melted
2 teaspoons grated lemon peel
3 drops yellow food coloring (optional)
⅔ cup sugar, divided
1 cup cold water
¼ cup cornstarch
⅛ teaspoon salt
¼ teaspoon vanilla

1. Preheat oven to 425°F. Bake pie crust according to package directions.

2. Separate eggs; discard 2 egg yolks. Mix lemon juice, butter, lemon peel and food coloring, if desired, in small bowl.

3. Reserve 2 tablespoons sugar. Combine water, remaining sugar, cornstarch and salt in medium saucepan; whisk until smooth. Heat over medium-high heat, whisking constantly, until mixture begins to boil. Reduce heat to medium. Continue to boil 1 minute, stirring constantly; remove from heat.

4. Stir ¼ cup boiling sugar mixture into egg yolks; whisk constantly until completely blended. Slowly whisk egg yolk mixture back into boiling sugar mixture. Cook over medium heat 3 minutes, whisking constantly. Remove from heat; stir in lemon juice mixture until well blended. Pour into baked pie crust.

5. Beat egg whites in large bowl with electric mixer at high speed until soft peaks form. Gradually beat in reserved 2 tablespoons sugar and vanilla; beat until stiff peaks form. Spread meringue over pie filling with rubber spatula, making sure meringue completely covers filling and touches edge of pie crust.

6. Bake 5 to 10 minutes or until lightly browned. Remove from oven; cool completely on wire rack. Cover with plastic wrap; refrigerate 8 hours or overnight until filling is firm and pie is chilled thoroughly. Cut into slices before serving.   *Makes 8 servings*

BAKE SALE

Table of Contents

Blissful Bars 194

Sinful Cakes 210

Cookie Jar 230

Tons of Muffins 246

Pies & Tarts 260

Acknowledgments 277

Index 278

Blissful Bars

Chip and Nut Brownie Bars

⅔ **cup butter or margarine**
½ **cup water**
2 **cups sugar**
2 **eggs**
1 **teaspoon vanilla extract**
1¼ **cups all-purpose flour**
1 **cup HERSHEY'S Cocoa**
½ **teaspoon baking powder**
¼ **teaspoon salt**
1⅓ **cups (8-ounce package) HERSHEY'S Premier Extra Dark Chocolate Chips**
1 **cup toasted almond slivers***

*To toast almonds: Heat oven to 350°F. Spread almonds in thin layer in shallow baking pan. Bake 8 to 10 minutes, stirring occasionally, until light golden brown; cool.

1. Heat oven to 350°F. Grease 13×9×2-inch baking pan.

2. Place butter and water in saucepan. Heat over medium heat until butter is melted. Stir in sugar. Add eggs and vanilla; beat with wooden spoon until well blended.

3. Stir together flour, cocoa, baking powder and salt. Gradually stir into sugar mixture, stirring until well blended. Stir in chocolate chips and almonds. Spread mixture in prepared pan.

4. Bake 35 to 40 minutes or until brownies begin to pull away from sides of pan. Cool completely in pan on wire rack. Cut into bars. *Makes about 36 bars*

Cobbled Fruit Bars

1½ cups apple juice
1 cup (6 ounces) chopped dried apricots
1 cup (6 ounces) raisins
1 package (6 ounces) dried cherries
1 teaspoon cornstarch
1 teaspoon ground cinnamon
1 package (about 18 ounces) yellow cake mix
2 cups old-fashioned oats
¾ cup (1½ sticks) butter, melted
1 egg

1. Combine apple juice, apricots, raisins, cherries, cornstarch and cinnamon in medium saucepan, stirring until cornstarch is dissolved. Bring to a boil over medium heat. Boil 5 minutes, stirring constantly. Remove from heat; cool to room temperature.

2. Preheat oven to 350°F. Line 15×10-inch jelly-roll pan with foil and spray lightly with cooking spray.

3. Combine cake mix and oats in large bowl; stir in butter (mixture may be dry and clumpy). Add egg; stir until well blended.

4. Press three-fourths dough mixture into prepared pan. Spread fruit mixture evenly over top. Sprinkle remaining dough mixture over fruit. Bake 25 to 30 minutes or until edges and top are lightly browned. Cool completely in pan on wire rack. Cut into bars.

Makes about 1 dozen bars

Fudgy Hazelnut Brownies

1 package DUNCAN HINES® Family-Style Chewy Fudge Brownie Mix
2 eggs
½ cup vegetable oil
¼ cup water
1 cup chopped toasted hazelnuts
1 cup semisweet chocolate chips
1 cup DUNCAN HINES® Creamy Home-Style Dark Chocolate Fudge
    Frosting
3 squares white chocolate, melted

continued on page 198

Fudgy Hazelnut Brownies, continued

1. Preheat oven to 350°F. Grease bottom only of 13×9-inch pan.

2. Combine brownie mix, eggs, oil and water in large bowl. Stir with spoon until well blended, about 50 strokes. Stir in hazelnuts and chocolate chips. Spread in prepared pan. Bake at 350°F for 25 to 30 minutes or until set. Cool completely.

3. Heat frosting in microwave oven at HIGH for 15 seconds or until thin; stir well. Spread over brownies. Spoon dollops of white chocolate over chocolate frosting; marble white chocolate through frosting. Cool completely. Cut into bars.

Makes 24 brownies

Double-Chocolate Pecan Brownies

- ¾ **cup all-purpose flour**
- ¾ **cup unsweetened cocoa powder**
- ½ **cup CREAM OF WHEAT® Hot Cereal (Instant, 1-minute, 2½-minute or 10-minute cook time), uncooked**
- ½ **teaspoon baking powder**
- 1¼ **cups sugar**
- ½ **cup (1 stick) butter, softened**
- 2 **eggs**
- 1 **teaspoon vanilla extract**
- ½ **cup semisweet chocolate chips**
- ½ **cup pecans, chopped**

1. Preheat oven to 350°F. Line 8-inch square baking pan with foil, extending foil over sides of pan; spray with nonstick cooking spray. Combine flour, cocoa, Cream of Wheat and baking powder in medium bowl; set aside.

2. Cream sugar and butter in large mixing bowl with electric mixer at medium speed. Add eggs and vanilla; mix until well combined.

3. Gradually add Cream of Wheat mixture; mix well. Spread batter evenly in pan, using spatula. Sprinkle chocolate chips and pecans evenly over top.

4. Bake 35 minutes. Let stand 5 minutes. Lift brownies from pan using aluminum foil. Cool completely before cutting.

Makes 9 brownies

Tip: For an even more decadent dessert, drizzle caramel sauce over the warm brownies and serve with mint chocolate chip ice cream.

Prep Time: 15 minutes
Start to Finish Time: 1 hour

Double-Chocolate Pecan Brownies

Double-Decker Confetti Brownies

¾ cup (1½ sticks) butter or margarine, softened
1 cup granulated sugar
1 cup firmly packed light brown sugar
3 eggs
1 teaspoon vanilla extract
2½ cups all-purpose flour, divided
2½ teaspoons baking powder
½ teaspoon salt
⅓ cup unsweetened cocoa powder
1 tablespoon butter or margarine, melted
1 cup "M&M's"® Semi-Sweet Chocolate Mini Baking Bits, divided

Preheat oven to 350°F. Lightly grease 13×9×2-inch baking pan; set aside. In large bowl, cream ¾ cup butter and sugars until light and fluffy; beat in eggs and vanilla. In medium bowl, combine 2¼ cups flour, baking powder and salt; blend into creamed mixture. Divide batter in half. Blend together cocoa powder and melted butter; stir into one half of the dough. Spread cocoa dough evenly into prepared baking pan. Stir remaining ¼ cup flour and ½ cup "M&M's"® Semi-Sweet Chocolate Mini Baking Bits into remaining dough; spread evenly over cocoa dough in pan. Sprinkle with remaining ½ cup "M&M's"® Semi-Sweet Chocolate Mini Baking Bits. Bake 25 to 30 minutes or until edges start to pull away from sides of pan. Cool completely. Cut into bars. Store in tightly covered container. *Makes 24 brownies*

Easy Microwave Brownies

1 cup granulated sugar
½ cup vegetable oil
¼ cup packed brown sugar
2 eggs
2 tablespoons corn syrup
1½ teaspoons vanilla
1 cup all-purpose flour
½ cup unsweetened cocoa powder
¼ teaspoon baking powder
¼ teaspoon salt
½ cup powdered sugar

Microwave Directions

1. Lightly grease 8-inch square microwavable dish.

2. Combine granulated sugar, oil, brown sugar, eggs, corn syrup and vanilla in large bowl. Combine flour, cocoa, baking powder and salt in medium bowl. Add flour mixture to sugar mixture; blend well. Spread batter in prepared dish.

3. Microwave on MEDIUM-HIGH (70%) 3 minutes. Rotate pan; microwave on MEDIUM-HIGH 3 minutes or until brownies begin to pull away from sides of pan and surface is dry. (If brownies are not done, rotate pan, turn and continue to microwave on MEDIUM-HIGH, checking for doneness at 30-second intervals.) Let brownies stand 20 minutes. When cool, sprinkle with powdered sugar and cut into squares.

Makes about 1 dozen brownies

Pumpkin Harvest Bars

1¾ **cups all-purpose flour**
  2 **teaspoons baking powder**
  1 **teaspoon grated orange peel**
  1 **teaspoon ground cinnamon**
  ½ **teaspoon salt**
  ½ **teaspoon ground nutmeg**
  ¼ **teaspoon ground ginger**
  ¼ **teaspoon ground cloves**
  ¾ **cup sugar**
  ½ **cup MOTT'S® Natural Apple Sauce**
  ½ **cup solid-pack pumpkin**
  1 **whole egg**
  1 **egg white**
  2 **tablespoons vegetable oil**
  ½ **cup raisins**

1. Preheat oven to 350°F. Spray 13×9-inch baking pan with nonstick cooking spray.

2. In small bowl, combine flour, baking powder, orange peel, cinnamon, salt, nutmeg, ginger and cloves.

3. In large bowl, combine sugar, apple sauce, pumpkin, whole egg, egg white and oil.

4. Add flour mixture to apple sauce mixture; stir until well blended. Stir in raisins. Spread batter into prepared pan.

5. Bake 25 to 30 minutes or until toothpick inserted in center comes out clean. Cool on wire rack 15 minutes; cut into 16 bars.

Makes 16 servings

Black Forest Bars

    1 package (about 18 ounces) dark chocolate cake mix
    ½ cup (1 stick) unsalted butter, melted
    1 egg
    ½ teaspoon almond extract
    1 cup sliced almonds, divided
    1 jar (about 16 ounces) maraschino cherries, well drained
    ½ cup semisweet chocolate chips

1. Preheat oven to 350°F. Line 13×9-inch baking pan with foil; set aside.

2. Combine cake mix, butter, egg and extract in large bowl with electric mixer at medium speed. Stir in ¾ cup almonds.

3. Press dough into bottom of prepared pan. Top evenly with cherries. Bake 20 to 25 minutes or until toothpick inserted into center comes out clean. Cool completely in pan on wire rack.

4. Place chocolate chips in small resealable food storage bag; seal bag. Microwave on HIGH 1 to 1½ minutes, kneading bag every 30 seconds until melted and smooth. Cut tiny corner from bag; drizzle chocolate over brownies. Sprinkle with reserved almonds. Cut into bars. *Makes about 2 dozen bars*

Prep Time: 10 minutes
Bake Time: 20 to 25 minutes

Caramel Chocolate Chunk Blondies

    1½ cups all-purpose flour
    1 teaspoon baking powder
    ½ teaspoon salt
    ¾ cup granulated sugar
    ¾ cup packed brown sugar
    ½ cup (1 stick) butter, softened
    2 eggs
    1½ teaspoons vanilla
    1½ cups semisweet chocolate chunks
    ⅓ cup caramel ice cream topping

continued on page 204

Caramel Chocolate Chunk Blondies, continued

1. Preheat oven to 350°F. Spray 13×9-inch baking pan with nonstick cooking spray.

2. Combine flour, baking powder and salt in medium bowl. Beat granulated sugar, brown sugar and butter in large bowl with electric mixer at medium speed until smooth and creamy. Beat in eggs and vanilla until well blended. Add flour mixture; beat at low speed until blended. Stir in chocolate chunks.

3. Spread batter evenly in prepared pan. Drop spoonfuls of caramel topping over batter; swirl into batter with knife.

4. Bake 25 minutes or until golden brown. Cool in pan on wire rack.

Makes about 2½ dozen blondies

Double Peanut Butter Paisley Brownies

  ½ **cup (1 stick) butter or margarine, softened**
  ¼ **cup REESE'S® Creamy Peanut Butter**
   1 **cup granulated sugar**
   1 **cup packed light brown sugar**
   3 **eggs**
   1 **teaspoon vanilla extract**
   2 **cups all-purpose flour**
   2 **teaspoons baking powder**
  ¼ **teaspoon salt**
  1⅔ **cups (10-ounce package) REESE'S® Peanut Butter Chips**
  ½ **cup HERSHEY'S Syrup or HERSHEY'S SPECIAL DARK® Syrup**

1. Heat oven to 350°F. Grease 13×9×2-inch baking pan.

2. Beat butter and peanut butter in large bowl. Add granulated sugar and brown sugar; beat well. Add eggs, one at a time, beating well after each addition. Blend in vanilla.

3. Stir together flour, baking powder and salt; mix into peanut butter mixture, blending well. Stir in peanut butter chips. Spread half of batter in prepared pan; spoon syrup over top. Carefully spread with remaining batter; swirl with metal spatula or knife for marbled effect.

4. Bake 35 to 40 minutes or until lightly browned. Cool completely in pan on wire rack. Cut into squares.

Makes about 36 brownies

Double Peanut Butter Paisley Brownies

Coconut Key Lime Bars

1 package (about 18 ounces) white cake mix
1 cup toasted coconut, plus additional for garnish
½ cup (1 stick) butter, melted
1 can (14 ounces) sweetened condensed milk
1 package (8 ounces) cream cheese, softened
Grated peel and juice of 3 limes
3 eggs

1. Preheat oven to 350°F. Line 13×9-inch pan with foil, leaving 2-inch overhang on sides.

2. Combine cake mix, coconut and butter in large bowl with electric mixer at medium speed until crumbly. Press mixture into bottom of prepared pan. Bake 12 minutes or until light golden brown.

3. Beat sweetened condensed milk, cream cheese, lime peel and juice in another large bowl at medium speed 2 minutes or until well blended; scrape down sides of bowl. Beat in eggs one at a time. Spread mixture evenly over crust.

4. Bake 20 minutes or until filling is set and edges are lightly browned. Sprinkle with toasted coconut. Cool completely in pan on wire rack.   *Makes about 2 dozen bars*

Prep Time: 10 minutes
Bake Time: 40 to 45 minutes

The full flavor of shredded coconut is released when it is toasted. Spread the coconut in an even layer on a baking sheet and place it in a preheated 350°F oven for 5 to 7 minutes. Peek at it after 5 minutes to make sure it is not in any danger of burning. If the coconut is fresh and moist, it will take a little longer to toast to a nice golden color than drier coconut.

Coconut Key Lime Bars

Chewy Peanut Butter Brownies

¾ cup (1½ sticks) butter, melted
¾ cup creamy peanut butter
1¾ cups sugar
2 teaspoons vanilla
4 eggs, lightly beaten
1¼ cups all-purpose flour
½ teaspoon baking powder
¼ teaspoon salt
¼ cup unsweetened cocoa powder

1. Preheat oven to 350°F. Grease 13×9-inch baking pan.

2. Beat butter and peanut butter in large bowl with electric mixer at low speed 3 minutes or until well blended. Add sugar and vanilla; beat until blended. Add eggs; beat until blended. Stir in flour, baking powder and salt just until blended. Reserve 1¾ cups batter. Stir cocoa into remaining batter.

3. Spread chocolate batter in prepared pan. Top with reserved batter. Bake 30 minutes or until edges begin to pull away from sides of pan. Cool completely in pan on wire rack. Cut into bars. *Makes 16 brownies*

Cran-Orange Oatmeal Bars

½ cup (1 stick) butter, softened
½ cup dried cranberries
1 egg
1 teaspoon grated orange peel, divided
3 tablespoons orange juice, divided
1 package (about 17 ounces) oatmeal cookie mix
1 cup powdered sugar

1. Preheat oven to 375°F. Spray 13×9-inch baking dish with nonstick cooking spray.

2. Combine butter, cranberries, egg, ½ teaspoon orange peel and 1 tablespoon orange juice in medium bowl. Stir in cookie mix until well blended. Spread batter evenly in prepared baking dish.

3. Bake 17 minutes or until light golden brown around edges. Cool completely in pan on wire rack. Blend powdered sugar and remaining 2 tablespoons orange juice in small bowl until smooth. Stir in remaining ½ teaspoon orange peel. Drizzle evenly over bars.
Makes about 2 dozen bars

Chewy Peanut Butter Brownies

Sinful Cakes

German Upside Down Cake

1½ cups shredded coconut
1 cup chopped pecans
1 container (16 ounces) coconut pecan frosting
1 package (about 18 ounces) German chocolate cake mix
1⅓ cups water
4 eggs
1 cup milk chocolate chips
⅓ cup vegetable oil
Whipped cream (optional)

1. Preheat oven to 350°F. Spray 13×9-inch glass baking dish with nonstick cooking spray.

2. Spread coconut evenly in prepared pan. Sprinkle pecans over coconut. Spoon frosting by tablespoonfuls over pecans. (Do not spread.)

3. Beat cake mix, water, eggs, chocolate chips and oil in large bowl with electric mixer at low speed 30 seconds. Beat at medium speed 2 minutes or until well blended and creamy. Pour batter into prepared pan, spreading carefully over frosting. Bake 35 to 40 minutes or until toothpick inserted into center comes out clean. Cool in pan 10 minutes; invert onto serving plate. Serve warm; top with whipped cream, if desired.

Makes 16 to 18 servings

Cherry-Almond Streusel Cake

Cake

  1½ **cups biscuit baking mix**
   ½ **cup milk**
   2 **eggs**
   2 **tablespoons granulated sugar**
   2 **tablespoons vegetable oil**
   1 **teaspoon vanilla**
   ¼ **teaspoon almond extract**
   ½ to ¾ **cup dried cherries***

Topping

   ½ **cup slivered almonds**
   ½ **cup oats**
   ⅓ **cup biscuit baking mix**
   ⅓ **cup packed dark brown sugar**
   ¼ **teaspoon ground cinnamon**
   3 **tablespoons cold butter, cubed**

Any dried fruit, such as cranberries or raisins, may be substituted.

1. Preheat oven to 375°F. Spray 8-inch round baking pan with nonstick cooking spray.

2. Combine 1½ cups baking mix, milk, eggs, granulated sugar, oil, vanilla and almond extract in medium bowl. Stir until well blended. Gently stir in cherries. Spread batter into prepared pan; set aside.

3. Combine almonds, oats, ⅓ cup baking mix, brown sugar and cinnamon in medium bowl. Cut in butter with pastry blender or two knives until butter is the size of peas.

4. Sprinkle topping evenly over batter. Bake 18 to 20 minutes or until toothpick inserted into center comes out almost clean. Let stand at least 30 minutes before serving.

Makes 12 servings

Cherry-Almond Streusel Cake

Chocolate Lemon Marble Cake

2½ **cups all-purpose flour**
1¾ **cups plus** ⅓ **cup sugar, divided**
  2 **teaspoons baking powder**
1¼ **teaspoons baking soda, divided**
  ½ **teaspoon salt**
  ⅓ **cup butter or margarine, softened**
  ⅓ **cup shortening**
  3 **eggs**
1⅔ **cups buttermilk or sour milk***
  2 **teaspoons vanilla extract**
  ⅓ **cup HERSHEY₅S Cocoa**
  ¼ **cup water**
  2 **teaspoons freshly grated lemon peel**
  ¼ **teaspoon lemon juice**
    Cocoa glaze (page 216)

To sour milk: Use 1 tablespoon plus 2 teaspoons white vinegar plus milk to equal 1⅔ cups.

1. Heat oven to 375°F. Grease and flour 12-cup fluted tube pan.**

2. Stir together flour, 1¾ cups sugar, baking powder, 1 teaspoon baking soda and salt in large bowl. Add butter, shortening, eggs, buttermilk and vanilla; beat on medium speed of electric mixer 3 minutes.

3. Stir together cocoa, remaining ⅓ cup sugar, remaining ¼ teaspoon baking soda and water; blend into ⅔ cup vanilla batter. Blend lemon peel and lemon juice into remaining vanilla batter; drop spoonfuls of lemon batter into prepared pan. Drop spoonfuls of chocolate batter on top of lemon batter; swirl with knife or metal spatula for marbled effect.

4. Bake 35 to 40 minutes or until wooden pick inserted in center comes out clean. Cool 15 minutes; remove from pan to wire rack. Cool completely. Glaze with Cocoa Glaze.   *Makes 16 to 18 servings*

**Cake may also be baked in 2 (9×5×3-inch) loaf pans. Bake 40 to 45 minutes or until wooden pick inserted in center comes out clean.*

continued on page 216

Chocolate Lemon Marble Cake

Chocolate Lemon Marble Cake, continued

Cocoa Glaze

¼ **cup HERSHEY®S Cocoa**
3 **tablespoons light corn syrup**
4 **teaspoons water**
½ **teaspoon vanilla extract**
1 **cup powdered sugar**

Combine cocoa, corn syrup and water in small saucepan; cook over medium heat, stirring constantly, until mixture thickens. Remove from heat; blend in vanilla and powdered sugar. Beat until smooth. *Makes about 1½ cups*

Sweet and Sour Brunch Cake

1 **package (16 ounces) frozen rhubarb, thawed and patted dry**
1 **cup packed brown sugar**
1 **tablespoon all-purpose flour**
1 **teaspoon ground cinnamon**
¼ **cup (½ stick) butter, diced**
1 **package (about 18 ounces) yellow cake mix** *without* **pudding in the mix**
1 **package (4-serving size) vanilla instant pudding and pie filling mix**
½ **cup water**
½ **cup vegetable oil**
4 **eggs**
⅔ **cup sour cream**

1. Preheat oven to 350°F. Spray 13×9-inch baking pan with nonstick cooking spray.

2. Spread rhubarb evenly in single layer in prepared pan. Combine brown sugar, flour and cinnamon in small bowl; mix well. Sprinkle evenly over rhubarb; dot with butter.

3. Beat cake mix, pudding mix, water, oil, eggs and sour cream in large bowl with electric mixer at low speed 1 minute. Beat at medium speed 2 minutes or until well blended and creamy. Pour batter into prepared pan, spreading carefully over rhubarb mixture.

4. Bake 40 to 50 minutes or until toothpick inserted into center comes out clean.
Makes 16 to 18 servings

Note: If frozen rhubarb is unavailable, substitute frozen unsweetened strawberries.

Sweet and Sour Brunch Cake

Oat-Apricot Snack Cake

1 (8 ounce) container plain yogurt (not fat free)
¾ cup packed brown sugar
½ cup granulated sugar
⅓ cup vegetable oil
1 egg
2 tablespoons milk
2 teaspoons vanilla
1 cup all-purpose flour
½ cup whole wheat flour
1 teaspoon baking soda
1 teaspoon cinnamon
½ teaspoon salt
2 cups old-fashioned oats
1 cup (about 6 ounces) chopped dried apricots
1 cup powdered sugar
2 tablespoons milk

1. Preheat oven to 350°F. Spray 13×9-inch baking pan with nonstick cooking spray. Stir yogurt, sugars, oil, egg, milk and vanilla in large bowl until thoroughly mixed.

2. Sift flours, baking soda, cinnamon and salt in medium bowl. Add dry ingredients to wet ingredients; mix well. Stir in oats and apricots until well mixed.

3. Spread batter in prepared pan. Bake 25 to 30 minutes or until toothpick inserted into center comes out clean. Cool completely in pan on wire rack.

4. Stir powdered sugar and milk in small bowl until smooth. Spoon glaze into small resealable food storage bag. Seal bag and cut ¼ inch from one corner; drizzle glaze over bars.   *Makes 16 to 18 servings*

Cranberry Pound Cake

1½ cups sugar
1 cup (2 sticks) unsalted butter
¼ teaspoon salt
¼ teaspoon ground mace
4 eggs
2 cups cake flour
1 cup chopped fresh or frozen cranberries

1. Preheat oven to 350°F. Grease and flour 9×5-inch loaf pan.

2. Beat sugar, butter, salt and mace in large bowl with electric mixer at medium speed until light and fluffy. Beat in eggs, one at a time, until well blended. Reduce speed to low; add flour, ½ cup at a time, scraping down bowl occasionally. Fold in cranberries.

3. Spoon batter into prepared pan. Bake 60 to 70 minutes or until toothpick inserted into center comes out clean. Cool in pan on wire rack 5 minutes. Run knife around edges of pan to loosen cake; cool additional 30 minutes. Remove from pan; cool completely on wire rack. *Makes 12 servings*

Note: You can make this cake when fresh or frozen cranberries aren't available. Cover 1 cup dried sweetened cranberries with hot water and let stand 10 minutes. Drain well before using.

Mandarin Orange Tea Cake

  1 package (16 ounces) pound cake mix
½ **cup plus 2 tablespoons orange juice, divided**
  2 eggs
¼ **cup milk**
  1 can (15 ounces) mandarin orange segments in light syrup, drained
¾ **cup powdered sugar**
  Grated peel of 1 orange

1. Preheat oven to 350°F. Grease 9-inch bundt pan.

2. Beat cake mix, ½ cup orange juice, eggs and milk in large bowl with electric mixer at medium speed 2 minutes or until light and fluffy. Fold in orange segments. Pour batter into prepared pan.

3. Bake 45 minutes or until golden brown and toothpick inserted near center comes out clean. Cool in pan 15 minutes on wire rack. Invert cake onto rack; cool completely.

4. Combine sugar, orange peel and remaining 2 tablespoons orange juice in small bowl; stir until smooth. Drizzle glaze over cake. Allow glaze to set about 5 minutes before serving. *Makes 16 servings*

Double Chocolate Chip Snack Cake

1 package (about 18 ounces) devil's food cake mix
    with pudding in the mix, divided
2 eggs
½ cup water
¼ cup vegetable oil
½ teaspoon cinnamon
1 cup semisweet chocolate chips, divided
¼ cup packed brown sugar
2 tablespoons butter, melted
¾ cup white chocolate chips

1. Preheat oven to 350°F. Grease 9-inch round cake pan. Reserve ¾ cup dry cake mix.

2. Beat remaining cake mix, eggs, water, oil and cinnamon in large bowl with electric mixer at medium speed 2 minutes. Remove ½ cup batter; reserve for another use.* Spread remaining batter in prepared pan; sprinkle with ½ cup semisweet chocolate chips.

3. Combine reserved cake mix and brown sugar in medium bowl. Stir in butter and remaining semisweet chocolate chips; mix well. Sprinkle mixture over batter in pan.

4. Bake 35 to 40 minutes or until toothpick inserted into center comes out clean and cake springs back when lightly touched. Cool cake in pan on wire rack 10 minutes. Remove to wire rack; cool completely.

5. Place white chocolate chips in medium resealable food storage bag; seal bag. Microwave on HIGH 10 seconds and knead bag gently. Repeat until chips are melted. Cut off ¼ inch from corner of bag; drizzle chocolate over cake. Let glaze set before cutting into wedges. *Makes 8 to 10 servings*

If desired, extra batter can be used for cupcakes. Pour batter into two foil baking cups placed on baking sheet. Bake at 350°F 18 to 20 minutes or until toothpick inserted into centers comes out clean.

Blueberry Cream Cheese Pound Cake

1 package (about 16 ounces) pound cake mix, divided
1½ cups fresh blueberries
4 ounces cream cheese, softened
2 eggs
¾ cup milk
    Powdered sugar (optional)

continued on page 222

Double Chocolate Chip Snack Cake

Blueberry Cream Cheese Pound Cake, continued

1. Preheat oven to 350°F. Grease 9×5-inch loaf pan.

2. Place ¼ cup cake mix in medium bowl; add blueberries and toss until well coated.

3. Beat cream cheese in large bowl with electric mixer at medium speed 1 minute or until light and fluffy. Add eggs, 1 at a time, beating well after each addition.

4. Add remaining cake mix alternately with milk, beginning and ending with cake mix, beating well after each addition. Beat 1 minute on medium speed or until light and fluffy. Fold blueberry mixture into batter. Pour batter into prepared pan.

5. Bake 55 to 60 minutes or until toothpick inserted into center comes out clean. Cool cake in pan on wire rack 10 minutes. Remove to rack to cool completely. Lightly sprinkle with powdered sugar, if desired. *Makes 12 servings*

Honey-Orange Spicecake

¾ **cup honey**
⅓ **cup oil**
¼ **cup orange juice**
2 **eggs**
1½ **cups all-purpose flour**
1 **teaspoon baking powder**
1 **teaspoon ground cinnamon**
½ **teaspoon baking soda**
¼ **teaspoon ground cloves**

Orange Syrup
¼ **cup honey**
¼ **cup orange juice**
2 **teaspoons freshly grated orange peel**

Using electric mixer, beat together honey, oil and orange juice; beat in eggs. Combine dry ingredients; gradually add to honey mixture, mixing until well blended.

Pour into lightly greased and floured 9×9-inch baking pan. Bake at 350°F for 25 to 30 minutes or until toothpick inserted in center comes out clean. Meanwhile, make syrup. In small saucepan, combine honey, orange juice and peel. Bring just to a boil. Remove cake from oven and immediately cut into squares.

Pour hot syrup evenly over cake in pan. Cool in pan on wire rack.

Makes 9 servings

Favorite recipe from **National Honey Board**

Honey-Orange Spicecake

Butterscotch Bundt Cake

1 package (about 18 ounces) yellow cake mix *without* pudding in the mix
1 package (4-serving size) butterscotch instant pudding and pie filling mix
1 cup water
3 eggs
2 teaspoons ground cinnamon
½ cup chopped pecans
  Powdered sugar (optional)

1. Preheat oven to 325°F. Spray 12-cup bundt pan with nonstick cooking spray.

2. Beat cake mix, pudding mix, water, eggs and cinnamon in large bowl with electric mixer at medium-high speed 2 minutes or until blended. Stir in pecans. Pour into prepared pan. Bake 40 to 50 minutes or until cake springs back when lightly touched. Cool in pan on wire rack 10 minutes. Invert cake onto serving plate; cool completely. Sprinkle with powdered sugar. *Makes 12 to 16 servings*

Pistachio Walnut Bundt Cake: Substitute white cake mix for yellow cake mix, pistachio pudding mix for butterscotch pudding and walnuts for pecans.

Topsy-Turvy Banana Crunch Cake

⅓ cup uncooked old-fashioned oats
 3 tablespoons packed brown sugar
 1 tablespoon all-purpose flour
¼ teaspoon ground cinnamon
 2 tablespoons butter
 2 tablespoons chopped pecans
 1 package (9 ounces) yellow cake mix *without* pudding in the mix
½ cup sour cream
½ cup mashed banana (about 1 medium)
 1 egg, slightly beaten
½ cup pecan halves (optional)

1. Preheat oven to 350°F. Lightly grease 8-inch square baking pan.

2. Combine oats, brown sugar, flour and cinnamon in small bowl. Cut in butter with pastry blender or two knives until crumbly. Stir in chopped pecans.

continued on page 226

Butterscotch Bundt Cake

Topsy-Turvy Banana Crunch Cake, continued

3. Beat cake mix, sour cream, banana and egg in medium bowl with electric mixer at low speed about 1 minute or until blended. Beat at medium speed 1 to 2 minutes or until smooth. Spoon half of batter into prepared pan; sprinkle with half of oat mixture. Top with remaining batter and oat topping. Sprinkle with pecan halves, if desired.

4. Bake 25 to 30 minutes or until toothpick inserted into center comes out clean. Cool completely in pan on wire rack.   *Makes 9 servings*

Chocolate Crispy Treat Cake

   1 package (about 18 ounces) chocolate fudge cake mix,
        plus ingredients to prepare mix
   1 cup semisweet chocolate chips
   ¼ cup light corn syrup
   ¼ cup (½ stick) butter
   ½ cup powdered sugar
   2 cups crisp rice cereal
   4 cups mini marshmallows (half of 10½-ounce package)

1. Preheat oven to 350°F. Grease bottom only of 13×9-inch pan. Prepare cake mix according to package directions; pour into prepared pan. Bake 28 minutes or until cake is almost done.

2. Meanwhile, heat chocolate chips, corn syrup and butter in medium saucepan over low heat, stirring frequently, until chocolate and butter are melted. Remove from heat; blend in powdered sugar. Gently stir in cereal until well blended.

3. Remove cake from oven; sprinkle marshmallows over top of cake in single layer. Return cake to oven; bake 2 to 3 minutes longer until marshmallows puff up slightly.

4. Spread chocolate cereal mixture over marshmallows. Let cake stand until set.
                                         Makes 16 to 18 servings

Note: This cake is best eaten within a day or two of baking. After two days the cereal will become soggy.

Chocolate Crispy Treat Cake

Easy Apple Butter Cake

1 package (about 18 ounces) yellow cake mix *without* pudding in the mix
1 package (4-serving size) vanilla instant pudding and pie filling mix
1 cup sour cream
1 cup apple butter
4 eggs
½ cup apple juice
¼ cup vegetable oil
1 teaspoon ground cinnamon
½ teaspoon ground nutmeg
½ teaspoon ground cloves
¼ teaspoon salt
　Powdered sugar (optional)

1. Preheat oven to 375°F. Spray 10-inch tube pan with nonstick cooking spray.

2. Beat cake mix, pudding mix, sour cream, apple butter, eggs, apple juice, oil, cinnamon, nutmeg, cloves and salt in large bowl with electric mixer at low speed 1 minute. Beat at medium speed 2 minutes or until well blended and fluffy. Pour batter into prepared pan.

3. Bake 45 to 50 minutes or until toothpick inserted near center comes out clean. Cool in pan on wire rack 20 minutes. Run sharp knife along edge of pan to release cake; invert cake onto serving plate. Cool completely.

4. Just before serving, if desired, place 9-inch paper doily over cake. Sift powdered sugar over doily; remove carefully. *Makes 12 servings*

A butter cake is done when it begins to pull away from the sides of the pan, the top springs back when lightly touched and a toothpick inserted into the center comes out clean and dry.

Cookie Jar

Chocolate Chunk Cookies

1⅔ **cups all-purpose flour**
⅓ **cup CREAM OF WHEAT® Hot Cereal (Instant, 1-minute,**
    2½-minute or 10-minute cook time), uncooked
½ **teaspoon baking soda**
¼ **teaspoon salt**
¾ **cup (1½ sticks) butter, softened**
½ **cup packed brown sugar**
⅓ **cup granulated sugar**
1 **egg**
1 **teaspoon vanilla extract**
1 **(11½-ounce) bag chocolate chunks**
1 **cup chopped pecans**

1. Preheat oven to 375°F. Lightly grease cookie sheets. Blend flour, Cream of Wheat, baking soda and salt in medium bowl; set aside.

2. Beat butter and sugars in large bowl with electric mixer at medium speed until creamy. Add egg and vanilla. Beat until fluffy. Reduce speed to low. Add Cream of Wheat mixture; mix well. Stir in chocolate chunks and pecans.

3. Drop by tablespoonfuls onto prepared cookie sheets. Bake 9 to 11 minutes or until golden brown. Let stand on cookie sheet 1 minute before transferring to wire racks to cool completely. *Makes 24 cookies*

Tip: For a colorful item to take to school bake sales, replace the chocolate chunks with multicolored candy-coated chocolate.

Prep Time: 15 minutes
Start to Finish Time: 35 minutes

Peanut Butter Blossoms

48 HERSHEY'S KISSES®ʙʀᴀɴᴅ **Milk Chocolates**
¾ **cup REESE'S® Creamy Peanut Butter**
½ **cup shortening**
⅓ **cup granulated sugar**
⅓ **cup packed light brown sugar**
 1 **egg**
 2 **tablespoons milk**
 1 **teaspoon vanilla extract**
1½ **cups all-purpose flour**
 1 **teaspoon baking soda**
½ **teaspoon salt**
   Granulated sugar

1. Heat oven to 375°F. Remove wrappers from chocolates.

2. Beat peanut butter and shortening with electric mixer on medium speed in large bowl until well blended. Add ⅓ cup granulated sugar and brown sugar; beat until fluffy. Add egg, milk and vanilla; beat well. Stir together flour, baking soda and salt; gradually beat into peanut butter mixture.

3. Shape dough into 1-inch balls. Roll in additional granulated sugar; place on ungreased cookie sheet.

4. Bake 8 to 10 minutes or until lightly browned. Immediately press a chocolate into center of each cookie; cookies will crack around edges. Remove to wire racks and cool completely. *Makes about 4 dozen cookies*

Be creative at your next bake sale. Try placing the home-baked cookies on a decorative plate or in a gift box filled with colored tissue. Cookies can also be wrapped back-to-back in pairs with clear or colored plastic wrap and tied with colorful ribbon.

Peanut Butter Blossoms

Coconut Clouds

1 package (about 16 ounces) confetti angel food cake mix
½ cup water
1½ cups sweetened flaked coconut
1¼ cups slivered almonds, divided

1. Preheat oven to 325°F. Line cookie sheets with parchment paper.

2. Beat cake mix and water in large bowl with electric mixer at medium-high speed 3 minutes or until fluffy. Add coconut and 1 cup almonds; beat until combined. Drop tablespoonfuls of dough 2 inches apart onto prepared cookie sheets. Sprinkle tops with remaining ¼ cup almonds.

3. Bake 18 to 20 minutes or until bottoms are golden brown. Cool 1 minute on cookie sheets. Remove to wire rack to cool completely.　　　*Makes 4 dozen cookies*

Prep Time: 10 minutes
Bake Time: 22 to 24 minutes

Chunky Oatmeal Raisin Cookies

1 package (about 18 ounces) yellow cake mix
1½ cups old-fashioned oats
½ cup all-purpose flour
2 teaspoons ground cinnamon
½ cup packed brown sugar
2 eggs
1 teaspoon vanilla
1 cup (2 sticks) unsalted butter, melted
1 cup raisins
1 cup walnut pieces, toasted

1. Preheat oven to 375°F. Line cookie sheets with parchment paper.

2. Combine cake mix, oats, flour and cinnamon in large bowl until well blended. Beat brown sugar, eggs and vanilla in medium bowl until well blended. Add egg mixture and melted butter to dry ingredients; stir until combined. Fold in raisins and walnuts.

3. Drop tablespoonfuls of dough 2 inches apart onto prepared cookie sheets. Bake 14 to 16 minutes or until bottoms are golden brown.　　　*Makes about 4 dozen cookies*

Prep Time: 15 minutes
Bake Time: 14 minutes

Coconut Clouds

Greek Date-Nut Swirls

    1 cup firmly packed dried figs
    1 cup firmly packed pitted dates
    1 cup coarsely chopped walnuts
   12 tablespoons granulated sugar, divided
    ½ cup water
  1¾ cups all-purpose flour
    2 teaspoons ground anise seeds
    ¼ teaspoon baking powder
    ¼ teaspoon baking soda
    ¼ teaspoon salt
    ½ cup (1 stick) unsalted butter, softened
    4 ounces cream cheese, softened
    1 egg yolk
    1 teaspoon vanilla

1. Combine figs, dates, walnuts, 3 tablespoons sugar and water in food processor or blender; process until smooth.

2. Stir together flour, anise, baking powder, baking soda and salt in medium bowl; set aside.

3. Beat butter, cream cheese and 3 tablespoons sugar with electric mixer at medium speed until light and creamy. Add egg yolk, vanilla and flour mixture; beat until soft dough forms. Form dough into disc; wrap tightly in plastic wrap. Refrigerate at least 2 hours or until firm.

4. Place sheet of waxed paper on smooth, dry surface. Roll dough into 13×10-inch rectangle with lightly floured rolling pin. Gently spread fig mixture in even layer over dough. Beginning on one long side, lift waxed paper to roll up dough jelly-roll style. Spread remaining 6 tablespoons sugar on another sheet of waxed paper; roll log in sugar. Wrap sugared log in plastic wrap; refrigerate until firm, at least 4 hours or overnight.

5. Preheat oven to 350°F. Line two cookie sheets with parchment paper. Cut log into ⅓-inch-thick slices (about 36 slices). Place 2 inches apart on prepared cookie sheets.

6. Bake 12 to 14 minutes or until cookies are pale golden brown. Cool 1 minute on cookie sheets; transfer to wire rack to cool completely. Store in airtight container.

Makes about 3 dozen cookies

Quick Peanut Butter Chocolate Chip Cookies

1 package DUNCAN HINES® Moist Deluxe® Classic Yellow Cake Mix
½ cup creamy peanut butter
½ cup (1 stick) butter or margarine, softened
2 eggs
1 cup milk chocolate chips

1. Preheat oven to 350°F. Grease baking sheets.

2. Combine cake mix, peanut butter, butter and eggs in large bowl. Beat at low speed with electric mixer until well blended. Stir in chocolate chips.

3. Drop by rounded teaspoonfuls onto prepared baking sheets. Bake at 350°F for 9 to 11 minutes or until lightly browned. Cool 2 minutes on baking sheets. Remove to cooling racks. *Makes about 4 dozen cookies*

Tip: Crunchy peanut butter can be substituted for creamy peanut butter.

Cinnamon-Sugar Knots

¼ cup granulated sugar
¾ teaspoon ground cinnamon
1 package (about 18 ounces) spice cake mix
1 package (8 ounces) cream cheese, softened

1. Preheat oven to 350°F. Combine sugar and cinnamon in small bowl; set aside.

2. Beat cake mix and cream cheese together in large bowl with electric mixer at medium speed until well blended.

3. Shape dough into 1-inch balls; roll each ball into log about 4 inches long. Gently coil dough and pull up ends to form "knot." Place about 1½ inches apart on ungreased cookie sheets. Sprinkle with cinnamon-sugar. Bake 10 to 12 minutes or until lightly browned at edges.

4. Cool 2 minutes on cookie sheets. Remove to wire rack. Serve warm or cool completely before serving. *Makes about 4 dozen cookies*

Prep Time: 15 minutes
Bake Time: 10 to 12 minutes

Almond Milk Chocolate Chippers

½ cup slivered almonds
1¼ cups all-purpose flour
½ teaspoon baking soda
½ teaspoon salt
½ cup (1 stick) butter, softened
½ cup packed light brown sugar
⅓ cup granulated sugar
1 egg
2 tablespoons almond-flavored liqueur
1 cup milk chocolate chips

1. Preheat oven to 350°F. To toast almonds, spread on baking sheet. Bake 8 to 10 minutes or until golden brown, stirring frequently. Remove almonds from sheet; cool.

2. *Increase oven temperature to 375°F.* Combine flour, baking soda and salt in small bowl.

3. Beat butter, brown sugar and granulated sugar in large bowl with electric mixer at medium speed 2 to 3 minutes or until creamy. Beat in egg until well blended. Beat in liqueur. Gradually add flour mixture, beating until well blended. Stir in chips and almonds.

4. Drop dough by rounded teaspoonfuls 2 inches apart onto ungreased cookie sheets.

5. Bake 9 to 10 minutes or until edges are golden brown. Cool 2 minutes on cookie sheets. Remove to wire racks to cool completely. Store tightly covered at room temperature or freeze up to 3 months. *Makes about 3 dozen cookies*

Caribbean Crunch Shortbread

1 cup (2 sticks) unsalted butter, softened
½ cup powdered sugar
2 tablespoons packed light brown sugar
¼ teaspoon salt
2 cups all-purpose flour
1 cup diced dried tropical fruit mix, such as pineapple, mango and papaya

1. Beat butter, sugars and salt in large bowl with electric mixer at medium speed until creamy. Add flour, ½ cup at a time, beating after each addition. Stir in dried fruit.

continued on page 240

Almond Milk Chocolate Chippers

Caribbean Crunch Shortbread, continued

2. Shape dough into 14-inch log. Wrap in plastic wrap; refrigerate 1 hour.

3. Preheat oven to 300°F. Cut log into ½-inch slices; place on ungreased cookie sheets. Bake 20 to 25 minutes or until cookies are set and lightly browned. Cool on cookie sheets 5 minutes. Remove to wire racks to cool completely.

Makes about 2 dozen cookies

Oatmeal Scotchies

- 1¼ **cups all-purpose flour**
- 1 **teaspoon baking soda**
- ½ **teaspoon salt**
- ½ **teaspoon ground cinnamon**
- 1 **cup (2 sticks) butter or margarine, softened**
- ¾ **cup granulated sugar**
- ¾ **cup packed brown sugar**
- 2 **eggs**
- 1 **teaspoon vanilla extract** *or* **grated peel of 1 orange**
- 3 **cups quick or old-fashioned oats**
- 1⅔ **cups (11-ounce package) NESTLÉ® TOLL HOUSE® Butterscotch Flavored Morsels**

PREHEAT oven to 375°F.

COMBINE flour, baking soda, salt and cinnamon in small bowl. Beat butter, granulated sugar, brown sugar, eggs and vanilla extract in large mixer bowl. Gradually beat in flour mixture. Stir in oats and morsels. Drop by rounded tablespoonfuls onto ungreased baking sheets.

BAKE for 7 to 8 minutes for chewy cookies or 9 to 10 minutes for crispy cookies. Cool on baking sheets for 2 minutes; remove to wire racks to cool completely.

Makes about 4 dozen cookies

Pan Cookie Variation: GREASE 15×10-inch jelly-roll pan. Spread dough into prepared pan. Bake for 18 to 22 minutes or until light brown. Cool completely in pan on wire rack. Makes 4 dozen bars.

Chocolate Cherry Gems

1 package (about 16 ounces) refrigerated sugar cookie dough
⅓ cup unsweetened Dutch process cocoa powder*
3 tablespoons maraschino cherry juice, divided
18 maraschino cherries, cut into halves
¾ cup powdered sugar

*Dutch process, or European-style, cocoa gives these cookies an intense chocolate flavor and a dark, rich color. Other unsweetened cocoa powders can be substituted, but the flavor may be milder and the color may be lighter.

1. Preheat oven to 350°F. Lightly grease cookie sheets. Let dough stand at room temperature about 15 minutes.

2. Beat dough, cocoa and 1 tablespoon cherry juice in large bowl until well blended. Shape dough into 36 (¾-inch) balls; place 2 inches apart on prepared cookie sheets. Flatten balls slightly; press cherry half into center of each ball.

3. Bake 9 to 11 minutes or until set. Cool 2 minutes on cookie sheets; remove to wire racks to cool completely.

4. Combine powdered sugar and remaining 2 tablespoons cherry juice in small bowl; whisk until smooth. Add additional juice, 1 teaspoon at a time, if necessary, to create medium-thick pourable glaze. Drizzle glaze over cooled cookies. Let stand until set.

Makes 3 dozen cookies

Nutty Oatmeal Raisin Chews

2 cups uncooked old-fashioned oats
1 cup all-purpose flour
1 cup packed brown sugar
1 cup golden or dark raisins
1 cup walnut chips or finely chopped walnuts
½ cup canola oil
3 egg whites
1 teaspoon vanilla
¼ teaspoon salt

continued on page 244

Chocolate Cherry Gems

Nutty Oatmeal Raisin Chews, continued

1. Preheat oven to 375°F. Lightly grease cookie sheets.

2. Place all ingredients in large bowl; beat until well blended. Drop dough by rounded tablespoonfuls 2 inches apart onto prepared cookie sheets.

3. Dampen fingers with cold water and flatten dough into 2-inch rounds. Bake 12 to 14 minutes or until cookies are golden but not brown. Cool on cookie sheet 3 minutes. Remove to wire racks to cool completely. Store in airtight container.

Makes 3½ to 4 dozen cookies

Peanut Butter & Banana Cookies

¼ **cup (½ stick) butter**
½ **cup mashed ripe banana**
½ **cup peanut butter**
¼ **cup frozen apple juice concentrate**
 1 **egg**
 1 **teaspoon vanilla**
 1 **cup all-purpose flour**
½ **teaspoon baking soda**
¼ **teaspoon salt**
½ **cup chopped salted peanuts**
   Whole salted peanuts (optional)

1. Preheat oven to 375°F. Grease cookie sheets.

2. Beat butter in large bowl until creamy. Add banana and peanut butter; beat until smooth. Blend in apple juice concentrate, egg and vanilla. Beat in flour, baking soda and salt. Stir in chopped peanuts.

3. Drop dough by rounded tablespoonfuls 2 inches apart onto prepared cookie sheets; top each with one whole peanut, if desired. Bake 8 minutes or until set. Cool completely on wire racks. Store in tightly covered container.

Makes 2 dozen cookies

To make apple juice from a partially used can of concentrate, measure the amount of remaining concentrate and then add 3 times that amount in water. Stir well and enjoy.

Tons of Muffins

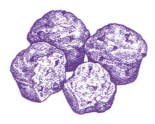

Raspberry Streusel Muffins

Streusel Topping

- 1 cup sugar
- ⅔ cup all-purpose flour
- 1 teaspoon cinnamon
- ¼ teaspoon salt
- ¼ cup pecan chips
- ½ cup (1 stick) butter, cut into small pieces
- 1 tablespoon milk

Raspberry Muffins

- 3 cups all-purpose flour
- 2 teaspoons baking powder
- ½ teaspoon salt
- ⅛ teaspoon ground cinnamon
- 1½ cups sugar
- ½ cup (1 stick) butter
- 2 eggs
- 1 teaspoon vanilla
- 1 cup sour cream
- 1½ pints fresh raspberries

1. Preheat oven to 350°F. Line 24 standard (2½-inch) muffin cups with paper baking cups.

2. For streusel topping, combine sugar, flour, cinnamon, salt and pecans in medium bowl. Cut in butter and milk with pastry blender or two knives until mixture resembles coarse crumbs. Set aside.

continued on page 248

Raspberry Streusel Muffins, continued

3. For muffins, whisk flour, baking powder, salt and cinnamon in medium bowl. Set aside.

4. Beat sugar and butter in large bowl with electric mixer at medium speed 2 to 3 minutes until light and fluffy. Add eggs, 1 at a time, beating well after each addition. Stir in vanilla. Mix in dry ingredients, alternating with sour cream. Gently fold in raspberries. Pour into muffin pans; sprinkle with streusel topping.

5. Bake 20 to 25 minutes or until toothpick inserted into centers comes out clean.

6. Cool pans on wire racks 10 minutes. Remove from pans; cool completely on wire racks.   *Makes 24 muffins*

Pumpkin Chocolate Chip Muffins

2½ **cups all-purpose flour**
  1 **tablespoon baking powder**
1½ **teaspoons pumpkin pie spice***
  ½ **teaspoon salt**
  1 **cup solid-pack pumpkin**
  1 **cup packed light brown sugar**
  ¾ **cup milk**
  6 **tablespoons butter, melted**
  2 **eggs**
  1 **cup semisweet chocolate chips**
  ½ **cup chopped walnuts**

Or substitute ¾ teaspoon ground cinnamon, ⅜ teaspoon ground ginger and scant ¼ teaspoon each ground allspice and ground nutmeg.

1. Preheat oven to 400°F. Line 18 standard (2½-inch) muffin cups with paper baking cups or spray with nonstick cooking spray.

2. Combine flour, baking powder, pumpkin pie spice and salt in large bowl. Beat pumpkin, brown sugar, milk, butter and eggs in medium bowl until well blended. Add pumpkin mixture, chocolate chips and walnuts to flour mixture; stir just until moistened. Spoon evenly into prepared muffin cups, filling two-thirds full.

3. Bake 15 to 17 minutes or until toothpick inserted into centers comes out clean. Cool in pans on wire racks 10 minutes. Remove from pans to rack; cool completely.   *Makes 18 muffins*

Pumpkin Chocolate Chip Muffins

Cranberry Pecan Muffins

1¾ cups all-purpose flour
½ cup packed light brown sugar
2½ teaspoons baking powder
½ teaspoon salt
¾ cup milk
¼ cup (½ stick) butter, melted
1 egg, beaten
1 cup chopped fresh cranberries
⅓ cup chopped pecans
1 teaspoon grated lemon peel

1. Preheat oven to 400°F. Grease 36 mini (1¾-inch) muffin cups.

2. Combine flour, brown sugar, baking powder and salt in large bowl. Combine milk, butter and egg in small bowl until blended; stir into flour mixture just until moistened. Fold in cranberries, pecans and lemon peel. Spoon evenly into prepared muffin cups.

3. Bake 15 to 17 minutes or until toothpick inserted into centers comes out clean. Remove from pans; cool on wire racks. *Makes 3 dozen mini muffins*

Red, White and Blue Muffins

2 cups all-purpose flour
¾ cup white chocolate chips
¾ cup *each* sweetened dried cranberries and dried blueberries
½ cup sugar
1 tablespoon baking powder
½ teaspoon salt
1 cup milk
½ cup (1 stick) butter, melted
1 egg, beaten
1 teaspoon vanilla

1. Preheat oven to 350°F. Grease 12 standard (2½-inch) muffin cups.

2. Combine flour, chocolate chips, dried berries, sugar, baking powder and salt in medium bowl. Combine milk, butter, egg and vanilla in large bowl. Add flour mixture to milk mixture; stir just until moistened. Spoon evenly into prepared muffin cups.

3. Bake 20 to 25 minutes or until toothpick inserted into centers comes out clean. Cool muffins 10 minutes on wire rack. *Makes 12 muffins*

Cranberry Pecan Muffins

Holiday Pumpkin Muffins

2½ **cups all-purpose flour**
  1 **cup packed light brown sugar**
  1 **tablespoon baking powder**
  1 **teaspoon ground cinnamon**
  ½ **teaspoon ground nutmeg**
  ½ **teaspoon ground ginger**
  ¼ **teaspoon salt**
  1 **cup solid-pack pumpkin (not pumpkin pie filling)**
  ¾ **cup milk**
  2 **eggs**
  6 **tablespoons butter, melted**
  ⅔ **cup roasted, salted pumpkin seeds, divided**
  ½ **cup golden raisins**

1. Preheat oven to 400°F. Grease 18 standard (2½-inch) muffin cups or line with paper baking cups.

2. Combine flour, brown sugar, baking powder, cinnamon, nutmeg, ginger and salt in large bowl. Stir pumpkin, milk, eggs and butter in medium bowl until well blended. Stir pumpkin mixture into flour mixture just until moistened. Stir in ⅓ cup pumpkin seeds and raisins. Spoon into prepared muffin cups, filling two-thirds full. Sprinkle remaining pumpkin seeds over muffin batter.

3. Bake 15 to 18 minutes or until toothpick inserted into center comes out clean. Cool in pans 10 minutes. Remove from pans and cool completely on wire racks. Store in airtight container. *Makes 18 muffins*

Carrot Pineapple Muffins

4 cups grated carrots (spooned, not packed, into cup)
1 cup granulated sugar
1 cup packed brown sugar
1 can (8 ounces) crushed pineapple in unsweetened pineapple juice, undrained
1 cup Dried Plum Purée (recipe follows) or prepared dried plum butter
4 egg whites
2 teaspoons vanilla
2 cups all-purpose flour
2 teaspoons baking soda
2 teaspoons ground cinnamon
½ teaspoon salt
¾ cup raisins (optional)

Preheat oven to 375°F. Coat eighteen 2¾-inch (⅓-cup capacity) muffin cups with vegetable cooking spray. In large bowl, beat carrots, sugars, pineapple, Dried Plum Purée, egg whites and vanilla until well blended. In medium bowl, combine flour, baking soda, cinnamon and salt. Add flour mixture to carrot mixture; mix just until blended. Stir in raisins. Spoon batter into prepared muffin cups, dividing equally. Bake in center of oven about 20 to 25 minutes or until springy to the touch and pick inserted into centers comes out clean. Cool in pans 15 minutes. Remove to wire racks. Serve warm. *Makes 18 muffins*

Plum Purée: Combine 1⅓ cups (8 ounces) pitted dried plums and 6 tablespoons hot water in container of food processor or blender. Pulse on and off until dried plums are finely chopped and smooth. Store leftovers in covered container in refrigerator for up to two months. Makes 1 cup.

Favorite recipe from **California Dried Plum Board**

Give Me S'more Muffins

2 cups graham cracker crumbs
⅓ cup sugar
⅓ cup mini semisweet chocolate chips
2 teaspoons baking powder
¾ cup milk
1 egg
24 milk chocolate candy kisses, unwrapped
2 cups mini marshmallows

1. Preheat oven to 350°F. Line 24 mini (1¾-inch) muffin cups with foil baking cups.

2. Combine graham cracker crumbs, sugar, chocolate chips and baking powder in medium bowl. Whisk milk and egg in small bowl; stir into crumb mixture until well blended. Spoon batter into prepared muffin cups, filling about half full. Press chocolate kiss into center of each cup. Press 4 marshmallows into top of each muffin around chocolate kiss.

3. Bake 10 to 12 minutes or until marshmallows are lightly browned. Cool muffins in pans on wire racks 10 minutes. Remove to racks; cool completely.

Makes about 2 dozen mini muffins

Berry Filled Muffins

1 package DUNCAN HINES® Bakery-Style Wild Maine Blueberry
    Muffin Mix
1 egg
½ cup water
¼ cup strawberry jam
2 tablespoons sliced natural almonds

1. Preheat oven to 400°F. Place 8 (2½-inch) paper or foil liners in muffin cups; set aside.

2. Rinse blueberries from Mix with cold water and drain.

3. Empty muffin mix into bowl. Break up any lumps. Add egg and water. Stir until moistened, about 50 strokes. Fill cups half full with batter.

4. Fold blueberries into jam. Spoon on top of batter in each cup. Spread gently. Cover with remaining batter. Sprinkle with almonds. Bake at 400°F for 17 to 20 minutes or until set and golden brown. Cool in pan 5 to 10 minutes. Loosen carefully before removing from pan.

Makes 8 muffins

Pineapple Carrot Raisin Muffins

   2 cups all-purpose flour
   1 cup sugar
1½ teaspoons baking powder
   1 teaspoon ground cinnamon
   1 can (8 ounces) DOLE® Crushed Pineapple, undrained
   2 eggs
  ½ cup (1 stick) butter or margarine, melted
   1 cup DOLE® Seedless or Golden Raisins
  ½ cup shredded DOLE® Carrots

• Combine flour, sugar, baking powder and cinnamon in large bowl.

• Add undrained pineapple, eggs, butter, raisins and carrots; stir just until blended.

• Spoon evenly into 36 mini muffin cups sprayed with nonstick vegetable cooking spray.

• Bake at 375°F., 15 to 20 minutes or until toothpick inserted in center comes out clean. Remove muffins from pans onto wire rack to cool.   *Makes 36 mini muffins*

For 2½-inch muffins: Spoon batter into 2½-inch muffin pans instead of mini muffin pans. Bake as directed for 20 to 25 minutes. Cool as directed.

Prep Time: 20 minutes
Bake Time: 20 minutes

Pineapple Carrot Raisin Muffins

Banana Peanut Butter Chip Muffins

 2 cups all-purpose flour
¾ cup sugar
 2 teaspoons baking powder
½ teaspoon baking soda
¼ teaspoon salt
 1 cup mashed ripe bananas (about 2 large)
½ cup (1 stick) butter, melted
 2 eggs, beaten
⅓ cup buttermilk
1½ teaspoons vanilla
 1 cup peanut butter chips
½ cup chopped peanuts

1. Preheat oven to 375°F. Grease 15 standard (2½-inch) muffins cups or line with paper baking cups.

2. Combine flour, sugar, baking powder, baking soda and salt in large bowl. Beat bananas, butter, eggs, buttermilk and vanilla in medium bowl until well blended.

3. Add banana mixture to flour mixture; stir just until blended. Gently fold in peanut butter chips. Spoon batter into prepared muffin cups, filling three-fourths full. Sprinkle with chopped peanuts.

4. Bake 20 minutes or until toothpick inserted into centers comes out clean. Cool 2 minutes in pan. Remove from pan; cool completely on wire racks. Serve warm or at room temperature. *Makes 15 muffins*

Substitute a mixture of chocolate and peanut butter chips for the peanut butter chips for a combination of three great flavors in one muffin.

Banana Peanut Butter Chip Muffins

Pies & Tarts

Honey Pumpkin Pie

1 can (16 ounces) solid pack pumpkin
1 cup evaporated low-fat milk
¾ cup honey
3 eggs, slightly beaten
2 tablespoons all-purpose flour
1 teaspoon ground cinnamon
½ teaspoon ground ginger
½ teaspoon rum extract
   Pastry for single 9-inch pie crust

Combine pumpkin, evaporated milk, honey, eggs, flour, cinnamon, ginger and rum in large bowl; beat until well blended. Pour into pastry-lined 9-inch pie plate. Bake at 400°F 45 minutes or until knife inserted near center comes out clean.

Makes 8 servings

Favorite recipe from **National Honey Board**

Chocolate Walnut Toffee Tart

2 cups all-purpose flour
1¼ cups plus 3 tablespoons sugar, divided
¾ cup (1½ sticks) cold butter, cut into pieces
2 egg yolks
1¼ cups whipping cream
1 teaspoon ground cinnamon
2 teaspoons vanilla
2 cups coarsely chopped walnuts
1¼ cups semisweet chocolate chips or chunks, divided

1. Preheat oven to 325°F. Place flour and 3 tablespoons sugar in food processor; pulse just until mixed. Scatter butter over flour mixture; process 20 seconds. Add egg yolks; process 10 seconds (mixture may be crumbly).

2. Transfer dough to ungreased 10-inch tart pan with removable bottom or 9- or 10-inch pie pan. Press dough firmly and evenly into pan. Bake 10 minutes or until surface is no longer shiny.

3. *Increase oven temperature to 375°F.* Place piece of foil in bottom of oven to catch any spills. Combine cream, remaining 1¼ cups sugar and cinnamon in large saucepan; bring to a boil over medium-high heat. Reduce heat to low; simmer 10 minutes, stirring frequently. Remove from heat and stir in vanilla.

4. Sprinkle walnuts and 1 cup chocolate chips evenly over partially baked crust. Pour cream mixture over top. Bake 35 to 40 minutes or until filling is bubbly and crust is lightly browned. Cool completely in pan on wire rack.

5. Place remaining ¼ cup chocolate chips in small resealable food storage bag. Microwave on HIGH 20 seconds; knead bag until chocolate is melted. Cut small hole in one corner of bag; drizzle chocolate over tart. *Makes 12 servings*

Note: Tart may be made up to 5 days in advance. Cover with plastic wrap and store at room temperature.

Prep Time: 25 minutes
Bake Time: 40 minutes

Chocolate Walnut Toffee Tart

Rustic Plum Tart

¼ **cup (½ stick) plus 1 tablespoon butter, divided**
 3 **cups plum wedges (about 6 plums, see Tip)**
¼ **cup granulated sugar**
½ **cup all-purpose flour**
½ **cup uncooked old-fashioned or quick oats**
¼ **cup packed brown sugar**
½ **teaspoon ground cinnamon**
¼ **teaspoon salt**
 1 **egg**
 1 **teaspoon water**
 1 **refrigerated pie crust (half of 15-ounce package)**
 1 **tablespoon chopped crystallized ginger**

1. Preheat oven to 425°F. Line baking sheet with parchment paper.

2. Melt 1 tablespoon butter in large skillet over high heat. Add plums; cook and stir about 3 minutes or until plums begin to break down. Stir in granulated sugar; cook 1 minute or until juices have thickened. Remove from heat; set aside.

3. Combine flour, oats, brown sugar, cinnamon and salt in medium bowl. Cut in remaining ¼ cup butter with pastry blender or two knives until mixture resembles coarse crumbs.

4. Beat egg and water in small bowl. Unroll pie crust on prepared baking sheet. Brush crust lightly with egg mixture. Sprinkle with ¼ cup oat mixture, leaving 2-inch border around edge of crust. Spoon plums over oat mixture, leaving juices in skillet. Sprinkle with ginger. Fold crust up around plums, overlapping as necessary. Sprinkle with remaining oat mixture. Brush edge of crust with egg mixture.

5. Bake 25 minutes or until golden brown. Cool slightly before serving.

Makes one 9-inch tart

For this recipe, use dark reddish-purple plums and cut the fruit into 8 wedges.

Apple-Cranberry Tart

1⅓ cups all-purpose flour
¾ cup plus 1 tablespoon sugar, divided
¼ teaspoon salt
2 tablespoons shortening
2 tablespoons butter
4 to 5 tablespoons ice water
½ cup boiling water
⅓ cup dried cranberries
1 teaspoon ground cinnamon
2 tablespoons cornstarch
4 medium baking apples
Vanilla frozen yogurt (optional)

1. Combine flour, 1 tablespoon sugar and salt in medium bowl. Cut in shortening and butter with pastry blender or two knives until mixture forms coarse crumbs. Mix in ice water, 1 tablespoon at a time, until mixture comes together and forms soft dough. Wrap in plastic wrap. Refrigerate 30 minutes.

2. Combine boiling water and cranberries in small bowl. Let stand 20 minutes or until softened.

3. Preheat oven to 425°F. Roll out dough on floured surface to ⅛-inch thickness. Cut into 11-inch circle. (Reserve any leftover dough scraps for decorating top of tart.) Ease dough into 10-inch tart pan with removable bottom, leaving ¼-inch dough above rim of pan. Prick bottom and sides of dough with tines of fork; bake 12 minutes or until dough begins to brown. Cool on wire rack. *Reduce oven temperature to 375°F.*

4. Combine remaining ¾ cup sugar and cinnamon in large bowl; mix well. Reserve 1 teaspoon mixture. Add cornstarch to bowl; mix well. Peel, core and thinly slice apples, adding pieces to bowl after sliced; toss well. Drain cranberries; add to apple mixture and toss well.

5. Arrange apple mixture attractively over dough. Sprinkle reserved 1 teaspoon sugar mixture evenly over top of tart. Place tart on baking sheet; bake 30 to 35 minutes or until apples are tender and crust is golden brown. Cool on wire rack. Remove side of pan; place tart on serving plate. Serve warm or at room temperature with frozen yogurt, if desired. *Makes 8 servings*

Apple-Cranberry Tart

Praline Pumpkin Tart

1¼ **cups all-purpose flour**
  1 **tablespoon granulated sugar**
 ¾ **teaspoon salt, divided**
 ¼ **cup shortening**
 ¼ **cup (½ stick) butter**
  3 to 4 **tablespoons cold water**
  1 **can (15 ounces) solid-pack pumpkin**
  1 **can (12 ounces) evaporated milk**
 ⅔ **cup packed brown sugar**
  2 **eggs**
  1 **teaspoon ground cinnamon, plus additional for garnish**
 ½ **teaspoon ground ginger**
 ¼ **teaspoon ground cloves**
    Praline Topping (page 269)
    Sweetened Whipped Cream (page 269)
    Pecan halves (optional)

1. For crust, combine flour, granulated sugar and ¼ teaspoon salt in large bowl. Cut in shortening and butter using pastry blender or two knives until mixture forms pea-sized pieces.

2. Sprinkle flour mixture with water, 1 tablespoon at a time. Toss with fork until mixture holds together. Shape into ball; wrap in plastic wrap. Refrigerate about 1 hour or until chilled.

3. Roll out dough on lightly floured surface into circle 1 inch larger than inverted 10-inch tart pan with removable bottom or 1½ inches larger than inverted 9-inch pie plate. Transfer dough to tart pan or pie plate; cover with plastic wrap and refrigerate 30 minutes.

4. Preheat oven to 400°F. Pierce crust with tines of fork at ¼-inch intervals. Line tart pan with foil; fill with dried beans, uncooked rice or ceramic pie weights.

5. Bake 10 minutes or until set. Remove from oven; gently remove foil lining and beans. Return to oven and bake 5 minutes or until very light brown. Cool completely on wire rack.

6. For filling, beat pumpkin, evaporated milk, brown sugar, eggs, cinnamon, remaining ½ teaspoon salt, ginger and cloves in large bowl with electric mixer at low speed. Pour into cooled tart crust. Bake 35 minutes.

7. Prepare Praline Topping. Sprinkle topping over center of tart, leaving 1½-inch rim around edge of tart. Bake 15 minutes or until knife inserted 1 inch from center comes out clean.

8. Cool completely on wire rack. Prepare Sweetened Whipped Cream and pipe decoratively around edge of pie. Sprinkle additional cinnamon over whipped cream. Garnish with pecan halves. *Makes 8 servings*

Praline Topping

⅓ **cup packed brown sugar**
⅓ **cup chopped pecans**
⅓ **cup uncooked quick oats**
1 **tablespoon butter or margarine, softened**

Place brown sugar, pecans and oats in small bowl. Cut in butter with pastry blender or two knives until coarse crumbs form. *Makes about 1 cup*

Sweetened Whipped Cream

1 **cup heavy cream**
2 **tablespoons powdered sugar**
½ **teaspoon vanilla**

Chill large bowl, beaters and cream before whipping. Place cream, powdered sugar and vanilla into chilled bowl and beat with electric mixer at high speed until soft peaks form. *Do not overbeat.* Refrigerate until ready to serve. *Makes about 2 cups*

Sweet 'n' Spicy Pecan Pie

Prepared pie crust for one 9-inch pie
3 **eggs**
1 **cup dark corn syrup**
½ **cup dark brown sugar**
¼ **cup (½ stick) butter or margarine, melted**
1 **tablespoon Original TABASCO® brand Pepper Sauce**
1½ **cups pecans, coarsely chopped**
Whipped cream (optional)

Preheat oven to 425°F. Place pie crust in 9-inch pie plate; flute edge of crust.

Beat eggs lightly in large bowl. Stir in corn syrup, brown sugar, butter and TABASCO® Sauce; mix well. Place pecans in prepared pie crust; pour filling over pecans. Bake 15 minutes.

Reduce oven to 350°F. Bake pie 40 minutes or until knife inserted 1 inch from edge comes out clean. Cool pie on wire rack. Serve with whipped cream, if desired.
Makes 8 servings

Apple & Cherry Pie

  2 cups all-purpose flour
  ½ cup plus 2½ tablespoons sugar, divided
  ½ teaspoon salt
  3 tablespoons butter or margarine
  3 tablespoons shortening
  1 tablespoon cider vinegar
  5 to 6 tablespoons ice water
  ½ cup dried cherries
  ¼ cup apple juice
  1 tablespoon cornstarch
2¼ teaspoons ground cinnamon, divided
  6 cups red baking apples, preferably Jonagold or Golden Delicious
  1 teaspoon vanilla
  1 egg white, well beaten

1. Combine flour, 2 tablespoons sugar and salt in large bowl. Cut in butter and shortening with pastry blender or two knives until mixture resembles coarse crumbs. Add vinegar and 4 tablespoons water, stirring with fork. Add additional water, 1 tablespoon at a time, until mixture forms soft dough. Divide dough into thirds. Shape 1 piece into disc; wrap in plastic wrap. Combine remaining 2 pieces dough, forming larger disc; wrap in plastic wrap. Refrigerate 30 minutes.

2. Preheat oven to 375°F. Combine cherries and apple juice in small microwavable bowl; microwave on HIGH 1½ minutes. Let stand 15 minutes to plump cherries. Combine ½ cup sugar, cornstarch and 2 teaspoons cinnamon in large bowl; mix well. Peel and thinly slice apples. Add to bowl with vanilla; toss to combine.

3. Coat 9-inch pie plate with nonstick cooking spray. Roll larger disc of dough to ⅛-inch thickness on lightly floured surface. Cut into 12-inch circle. Transfer pastry to prepared pie plate. Spoon apple mixture into pastry. Roll smaller disc of dough to ⅛-inch thickness. Cut dough into ½-inch strips. Place strips over filling and weave into lattice design. Trim ends of lattice strips; push edge of lower crust over ends of lattice strips. Seal and flute edge.

4. Brush pastry with egg white. Combine remaining ½ tablespoon sugar and remaining ¼ teaspoon cinnamon; sprinkle over pie. Bake 45 to 50 minutes or until apples are tender and crust is golden brown. Cool 30 minutes. Serve warm or at room temperature.   Makes 8 servings

Tip: If the pie crust is browning too quickly, cover the edges with strips of aluminum foil. Or, cut the bottom out of a foil pie pan and invert it over the pie.

Cherry Frangipane Tart

1 unbaked (9-inch) pie crust
⅔ cup slivered almonds
½ cup all-purpose flour
¼ cup powdered sugar
½ cup (1 stick) butter, softened
2 eggs
1¾ cups pitted frozen sweet cherries

1. Preheat oven to 450°F. Line tart pan with pie dough; cover with parchment paper. Fill with dried beans or pie weights and bake 10 minutes. Remove from oven. Carefully remove paper and weights. *Reduce oven temperature to 350°F.*

2. Combine almonds, flour and powdered sugar in bowl of food processor. Process until fine. Add butter; pulse to blend. Add eggs, one at a time, while processor is running.

3. Pour batter into baked crust; smooth top. Sprinkle with cherries. Bake about 35 minutes or until firm. Let cool completely in pan. *Makes 6 to 8 servings*

Spicy Pumpkin Pie

Pie pastry for single 9-inch pie crust
1 can (16 ounces) solid-pack pumpkin (not pumpkin pie filling)
¾ cup packed light brown sugar
2 teaspoons ground cinnamon
¾ teaspoon ground ginger
½ teaspoon ground nutmeg
¼ teaspoon salt
⅛ teaspoon ground cloves
4 eggs, lightly beaten
1½ cups light cream or half-and-half
1 teaspoon vanilla

1. Preheat oven to 400°F. Roll pie pastry on lightly floured surface to form 13-inch circle. Fit into 9-inch pie plate. Trim edges; flute.

2. Combine pumpkin and brown sugar in large bowl; mix well. Stir in cinnamon, ginger, nutmeg, salt and cloves. Add eggs; mix well. Gradually stir in cream and vanilla; mix until combined. Pour pumpkin mixture into unbaked pie crust.

3. Bake 40 to 45 minutes or until knife inserted near center comes out clean. Cool on wire rack. *Makes one 9-inch pie*

Cherry Frangipane Tart

Classic Apple Pie

1 package (15 ounces) refrigerated pie crusts (2 crusts)
6 cups sliced Granny Smith, Crispin or other firm-fleshed apples
½ cup sugar
1 tablespoon cornstarch
2 teaspoons lemon juice
½ teaspoon *each* ground cinnamon and vanilla
⅛ teaspoon *each* salt, ground nutmeg and ground cloves
1 tablespoon whipping cream

1. Preheat oven to 350°F. Unfold one pie crust; press into 9-inch pie dish. (Keep remaining pie crust in refrigerator while preparing apples.)

2. Combine apples, sugar, cornstarch, lemon juice, cinnamon, vanilla, salt, nutmeg and cloves in large bowl; mix well. Pour into prepared crust. Place second crust over apples; crimp around edge to seal crusts together.

3. Cut 4 slits in top crust; brush top crust with cream. Bake 40 minutes or until apples are tender and crust is golden brown. Cool slightly before serving.

Makes 8 servings

Country Pecan Pie

Pie pastry for single 9-inch pie crust
1¼ cups dark corn syrup
4 eggs
½ cup packed light brown sugar
¼ cup (½ stick) butter or margarine, melted
2 teaspoons all-purpose flour
1½ teaspoons vanilla
1½ cups pecan halves

1. Preheat oven to 350°F. Roll pastry on lightly floured surface to form 13-inch circle. Fit into 9-inch pie plate. Trim edges; flute. Set aside.

2. Beat corn syrup, eggs, brown sugar and butter in large bowl with electric mixer at medium speed 2 to 3 minutes or until well blended. Stir in flour and vanilla until blended. Pour into unbaked pie crust. Arrange pecans on top.

3. Bake 40 to 45 minutes until center of filling is puffed and golden brown. Cool completely on wire rack. Garnish as desired.

Makes one 9-inch pie

Classic Apple Pie

Old-Fashioned Pumpkin Pie

1 cup sugar
1 tablespoon all-purpose flour
1 tablespoon WATKINS® Pumpkin Pie Spice
½ teaspoon salt
3 eggs
1½ cups canned pumpkin or mashed, cooked pumpkin
1 cup evaporated milk
1 unbaked 9-inch pie crust
Vanilla Whipped Cream (optional, recipe follows)

Preheat oven to 400°F. Combine sugar, flour, pumpkin pie spice and salt in large bowl; beat in eggs until well blended. Stir in pumpkin and evaporated milk until smooth. Pour into pie crust. Bake for 50 minutes or until knife inserted into center comes out clean. Serve with Vanilla Whipped Cream, if desired.   *Makes 10 servings*

Vanilla Whipped Cream (Creme Chantilly)

1 cup heavy whipping cream
2 to 4 tablespoons powdered sugar (depending on sweetness desired)
1 teaspoon WATKINS® Vanilla

Chill small bowl and beaters of electric mixer in refrigerator (chill in freezer if in a hurry). Beat cream in chilled bowl until it begins to thicken. Add sugar and vanilla; beat until stiff. Do not overbeat.   *Makes 2 cups*

If you don't want to make real whipped cream, you can improve flavor of the store-bought variety by adding 1 teaspoon WATKINS® Vanilla to 2 cups frozen, thawed whipped topping.

The publisher would like to thank the companies and organizations listed below for the use of their recipes and photographs in this publication.

ACH Food Companies, Inc.

California Dried Plum Board

Campbell Soup Company

Cherry Marketing Institute

Cream of Wheat® Cereal

Dole Food Company, Inc.

Duncan Hines® and Moist Deluxe® are registered trademarks of Pinnacle Foods Corp.

Filippo Berio® Olive Oil

The Hershey Company

Hillshire Farm®

Idaho Potato Commission

Jennie-O Turkey Store, LLC

©2009 Kraft Foods, KRAFT, KRAFT Hexagon Logo, PHILADELPHIA AND PHILADELPHIA Logo are registered trademarks of Kraft Foods Holdings, Inc. All rights reserved.

© Mars, Incorporated 2009

McIlhenny Company (TABASCO® brand Pepper Sauce)

Michigan Apple Committee

Mott's® is a registered trademark of Mott's, LLP

National Fisheries Institute

National Honey Board

Nestlé USA

Norseland, Inc.

North Dakota Wheat Commission

Ortega®, A Division of B&G Foods, Inc.

Reckitt Benckiser Inc.

RED STAR® Yeast, a product of Lasaffre Yeast Corporation

Riviana Foods Inc.

Roman Meal® Company

Sargento® Foods Inc.

Sonoma® Dried Tomatoes

Unilever

USA Rice Federation®

Veg•All®

Watkins Incorporated

A

Almond
Almond and Vanilla Green Beans, 170
Almond Milk Chocolate Chippers, 238
Black Forest Bars, 202
Cherry-Almond Streusel Cake, 212
Cherry Frangipane Tart, 272
Chip and Nut Brownie Bars, 194
Coconut Clouds, 234
Creamy Chile and Chicken Casserole, 56
English Bath Buns, 134

Apple
Apple & Cherry Pie, 270
Apple-Cranberry Tart, 266
Apple-Pomegranate Crisp, 190
Aunt Marilyn's Cinnamon French Toast
    Casserole, 2
Baked Apples with Cinnamon Chip
    Streusel, 186
Classic Apple Pie, 274
Cobbled Fruit Bars, 196
Easy Apple Butter Cake, 228
Ham 'n' Apple Breakfast Casserole Slices, 4
Pumpkin Harvest Bars, 201
Roasted Sweet Potato Salad, 71

Apricots
Cobbled Fruit Bars, 196
Oat-Apricot Snack Cake, 218

Artichokes
Crab-Artichoke Casserole, 84
Spinach Artichoke Gratin, 160
Asian Beef Stew, 112
Aunt Marilyn's Cinnamon French Toast
    Casserole, 2

B

Bacon
Bacon and Maple Grits Puff, 18
Easy Cheesy Bacon Bread, 122
Loaded, Baked Potato Salad, 70
Nine-Layer Salad, 68
Spinach Sensation, 16
Baked Apples with Cinnamon Chip
    Streusel, 186
Baked Bow-Tie Pasta in Mushroom Cream
    Sauce, 30
Baked Potato Soup, 107
Baked Ravioli with Pumpkin Sauce, 34

Baked Red Snappers with Veg•All®, 82
Banana Peanut Butter Chip Muffins, 258

Bananas
Banana Peanut Butter Chip Muffins, 258
Peanut Butter & Banana Cookies, 244
Topsy-Turvy Banana Crunch Cake, 224

Bars
Black Forest Bars, 202
Caramel Chocolate Chunk Blondies, 202
Chip and Nut Brownie Bars, 194
Cobbled Fruit Bars, 196
Coconut Key Lime Bars, 206
Cran-Orange Oatmeal Bars, 208
Pumpkin Harvest Bars, 201

Beans, Black
Black Bean Flautas with Charred
    Tomatillo Salsa, 32
Fiesta Pasta Salad, 72
Fresh Lime and Black Bean Soup, 98
Southwestern Chicken and Black Bean
    Skillet, 154
Spicy Chicken Casserole with Corn
    Bread, 52
Tortilla Beef Casserole, 52

Beans, Green
Almond and Vanilla Green Beans, 170
Green Bean Casserole, 162
Italian Hillside Garden Soup, 108
Shrimp Primavera Pot Pie, 90
Spanish Stewed Tomatoes, 167
Very Verde Green Bean Salad, 62

Beef (*see also* **Beef, Ground**)
Asian Beef Stew, 112
Old-Fashioned Cabbage Rolls, 51
Savory Garlic Steak with Charred Tomato
    Salsa, 142
Sicilian Steak Pinwheels, 146
Southwestern Enchiladas, 44
Steak Diane with Cremini Mushrooms,
    152
Tortilla Beef Casserole, 52

Beef, Ground
Cheese-Stuffed Meat Loaf, 148
Chorizo Chili, 108
Cousin Arlene's Spaghetti Lasagna, 50
It's a Keeper Casserole, 40
Lasagna Supreme, 60
Layered Pasta Casserole, 54
Mexican Tossed Layer Casserole, 44

Beef, Ground (*continued*)
Old-Fashioned Cabbage Rolls, 51
Old-Fashioned Meat Loaf, 138
Porcupine Meatballs, 144
Rainbow Casserole, 48
Bell Peppers
Baked Red Snappers with Veg•All®, 82
Creamy Chile and Chicken Casserole, 56
Delicious Ham & Cheese Puff Pie, 20
Easy Cheesy Bacon Bread, 122
Hash Brown Casserole, 8
Italian Hillside Garden Soup, 108
Italian Vegetable Strata, 34
Louisiana Gumbo, 100
Mediterranean-Style Tuna Noodle
Casserole, 90
Pork Chops with Cranberry-Jalapeño
Relish, 150
Pounceole Salad, 76
Quinoa-Stuffed Tomatoes, 26
Roasted Vegetable Salad with Capers and
Walnuts, 64
Sausage Pizza Pie Casserole, 42
Shrimp Creole, 96
Shrimp Primavera Pot Pie, 90
Southwestern Chicken and Black Bean
Skillet, 154
Southwestern Corn and Pasta Casserole, 38
Southwest Pasta Salad, 68
Spicy Citrus Pork with Pineapple Salsa,
156
Veggie-Stuffed Portobello Mushrooms, 22
Berry
Apple-Cranberry Tart, 266
Berry Filled Muffins, 254
Biscuit and Sausage Bake, 8
Blueberry Cream Cheese Pound
Cake, 220
Cranberry Coffee Cake, 13
Cranberry Pecan Muffins, 250
Cranberry Pound Cake, 218
Cran-Orange Oatmeal Bars, 208
Cran-Raspberry Gelatin Salad, 66
Pork Chops with Cranberry-Jalapeño
Relish, 150
Raspberry Streusel Muffins, 246
Red, White and Blue Muffins, 250
Roasted Sweet Potato Salad, 71
Rustic Cranberry-Pear Galette, 188

Berry (*continued*)
Tapioca Fruit Salad, 78
Wild Rice, Mushroom and Cranberry
Dressing, 28
Biscuit and Sausage Bake, 8
Black Bean Flautas with Charred Tomatillo
Salsa, 32
Black Forest Bars, 202
Blueberry Cream Cheese Pound Cake, 220
Breads, 118–135
Breakfast Bake, 4
Broccoli
Crustless Salmon & Broccoli Quiche, 86
Spicy Jac Mac & Cheese with Broccoli, 26
Veggie and Cheese Manicotti, 30
Brownies
Double-Chocolate Pecan Brownies, 198
Double-Decker Confetti Brownies, 200
Double Peanut Butter Paisley Brownies,
204
Chewy Peanut Butter Brownies, 208
Easy Microwave Brownies, 200
Fudgy Hazelnut Brownies, 196
Brunch Eggs Olé, 12
Butterscotch
Butterscotch Bundt Cake, 224
Oatmeal Scotchies, 240

C
Cabbage
Hearty Vegetable Stew, 112
Old-Fashioned Cabbage Rolls, 51
Cakes, 210–229 (*see also* **Coffee Cakes**)
Carrot Cake with Black Walnut Frosting,
176
Chocolate Mousse Cake Roll, 184
Candied Sweet Potatoes, 172
Caramel Chocolate Chunk Blondies, 202
Caramelized Onion Tart, 24
Caribbean Crunch Shortbread, 238
Carrot Cake with Black Walnut Frosting, 176
Carrot Pineapple Muffins, 253
Carrots
Asian Beef Stew, 112
Carrot Cake with Black Walnut Frosting,
176
Carrot Pineapple Muffins, 253
Chutney Glazed Carrots, 172
Glazed Parsnips and Carrots, 164

Carrots (continued)
Hearty Vegetable Stew, 112
Lemon Shrimp, 82
Nine-Layer Salad, 68
Pineapple Carrot Raisin Muffins, 256
Pork and Corn Bread Stuffing Casserole, 58
Veggie and Cheese Manicotti, 30
Casseroles
Aunt Marilyn's Cinnamon French Toast
Casserole, 2
Bacon and Maple Grits Puff, 18
Baked Bow-Tie Pasta in Mushroom Cream
Sauce, 30
Baked Ravioli with Pumpkin Sauce, 34
Baked Red Snappers with Veg●All®, 82
Biscuit and Sausage Bake, 8
Black Bean Flautas with Charred
Tomatillo Salsa, 32
Breakfast Bake, 4
Brunch Eggs Olé, 12
Candied Sweet Potatoes, 172
Cousin Arlene's Spaghetti Lasagna, 50
Crab-Artichoke Casserole, 84
Creamy Chile and Chicken Casserole, 56
Crunchy Veg●All® Tuna Casserole, 96
Crustless Salmon & Broccoli Quiche, 86
Delicious Ham & Cheese Puff Pie, 20
French Toast Strata, 10
Green Bean Casserole, 162
Ham 'n' Apple Breakfast Casserole Slices, 4
Hash Brown Casserole, 8
Heartland Chicken Casserole, 46
Italian Vegetable Strata, 34
It's a Keeper Casserole, 40
Lasagna Supreme, 60
Layered Pasta Casserole, 54
Lemon Shrimp, 82
Mediterranean-Style Tuna Noodle
Casserole, 90
Mexican Tossed Layer Casserole, 44
Old-Fashioned Cabbage Rolls, 51
Old-Fashioned Turkey Pot Pie, 42
Paella, 94
Parmesan Vegetable Bake, 31
Pork and Corn Bread Stuffing Casserole, 58
Rainbow Casserole, 48
Sausage Pizza Pie Casserole, 42
Shrimp Creole, 96
Shrimp Primavera Pot Pie, 90

Casseroles (continued)
Southwestern Corn and Pasta Casserole, 38
Southwestern Enchiladas, 44
Spicy Chicken Casserole with Corn Bread,
52
Spicy Jac Mac & Cheese with Broccoli, 26
Spinach Artichoke Gratin, 160
Spinach Sensation, 16
Summer Sausage 'n' Egg Wedges, 14
Surimi Seafood-Zucchini Frittata with
Fresh Tomato Sauce, 88
Tortilla Beef Casserole, 52
Tuna Tomato Casserole, 80
Turkey and Mushroom Wild Rice
Casserole, 48
Veggie and Cheese Manicotti, 30
Wild Rice, Mushroom and Cranberry
Dressing, 28
Cheesecakes
Chocolate Vanilla Swirl Cheesecake, 174
New York-Style Sour Cream-Topped
Cheesecake, 182
Cheese-Stuffed Meat Loaf, 148
Cherry
Apple & Cherry Pie, 270
Black Forest Bars, 22
Cherry-Almond Streusel Cake, 212
Cherry Crisp, 178
Cherry Frangipane Tart, 272
Chocolate Cherry Gems, 242
Cobbled Fruit Bars, 196
Chewy Peanut Butter Brownies, 208
Chicken
Creamy Chile and Chicken Casserole, 56
Green Chile Chicken Soup with Tortilla
Dumplings, 116
Grilled Corn & Chicken Soup, 110
Heartland Chicken Casserole, 46
Hearty Chicken Chili, 102
Nutty Oven-Fried Chicken Drumsticks,
146
Oven Barbecue Chicken, 142
Paella, 94
Southern Buttermilk Fried Chicken, 136
Southwestern Chicken and Black Bean
Skillet, 154
Spicy Chicken Casserole with Corn Bread,
52
Spicy Squash & Chicken Soup, 106

Chili
  Chorizo Chili, 108
  Hearty Chicken Chili, 102
Chip and Nut Brownie Bars, **194**
Chocolate (*see also* **Chocolate Chips**)
  Black Forest Bars, 202
  Chewy Peanut Butter Brownies, 208
  Chip and Nut Brownie Bars, 194
  Chocolate Cherry Gems, 242
  Chocolate Crispy Treat Cake, 226
  Chocolate Lemon Marble Cake, 214
  Chocolate Mousse Cake Roll, 184
  Chocolate Vanilla Swirl Cheesecake, 174
  Cocoa Glaze, 216
  Double Chocolate Chip Snack Cake, 220
  Double-Chocolate Pecan Brownies, 198
  Double Peanut Butter Paisley Brownies, 204
  Easy Microwave Brownies, 200
  Fudgy Hazelnut Brownies, 196
  German Upside Down Cake, 210
  Hershey's Brownies with Peanut Butter
    Frosting, 180
Chocolate Chips
  Almond Milk Chocolate Chippers, 238
  Black Forest Bars, 22
  Caramel Chocolate Chunk Blondies, 202
  Chip and Nut Brownie Bars, 194
  Chocolate Chunk Coffee Cake, 14
  Chocolate Chunk Cookies, 230
  Chocolate Crispy Treat Cake, 226
  Chocolate Croissant Pudding, 176
  Chocolate Mousse Filling, 185
  Chocolate Walnut Toffee Tart, 262
  Double Chocolate Chip Snack Cake, 220
  Double-Chocolate Pecan Brownies, 198
  Double-Decker Confetti Brownies, 200
  Fudgy Hazelnut Brownies, 196
  German Upside Down Cake, 210
  Give Me S'more Muffins, 254
  Peanut Butter Blossoms, 232
  Pumpkin Chocolate Chip Muffins, 248
  Quick Peanut Butter Chocolate Chip
    Cookies, 237
Chocolate Chunk Coffee Cake, 14
Chocolate Chunk Cookies, 230
Chocolate Crispy Treat Cake, 226
Chocolate Croissant Pudding, 176
Chocolate Lemon Marble Cake, 214
Chocolate Mousse Cake Roll, 184

Chocolate Mousse Filling, 185
Chocolate Vanilla Swirl Cheesecake, 174
Chocolate Walnut Toffee Tart, 262
Chorizo Chili, 108
Chunky Oatmeal Raisin Cookies, 234
Chunky Ranch Potatoes, 164
Chutney Glazed Carrots, 172
Cinnamon-Sugar Knots, 237
Clams: Paella, 94
Classic Apple Pie, 274
Cobbled Fruit Bars, 196
Cocoa Glaze, 216
Coconut
  Coconut Clouds, 234
  Coconut Key Lime Bars, 206
  German Upside Down Cake, 210
Coffee Cakes
  Chocolate Chunk Coffee Cake, 14
  Cranberry Coffee Cake, 13
  Nutty Toffee Coffee Cake, 18
  Pineapple Coffee Cake, 6
Cookies, 230–245 (*see also* **Bars**)
Corn
  Fiesta Pasta Salad, 72
  Grilled Corn & Chicken Soup, 110
  Jerk Pork and Sweet Potato Stew, 106
  Nine-Layer Salad, 68
  Pounceole Salad, 76
  Rio Bravo Rice-Stuffed Poblanos, 36
  Salsa-Buttered Corn on the Cob, 160
  Southwestern Corn and Pasta Casserole, 38
  Southwest Pasta Salad, 68
  Spicy Chicken Casserole with Corn Bread,
    52
  Tortilla Beef Casserole, 52
Country Pecan Pie, 274
Cousin Arlene's Spaghetti Lasagna, 50
Crab
  Crab-Artichoke Casserole, 84
  Creamy Alfredo Seafood Lasagna, 84
  Surimi Seafood-Zucchini Frittata with
    Fresh Tomato Sauce, 88
Cranberry Coffee Cake, 13
Cranberry Pecan Muffins, 250
Cranberry Pound Cake, 218
Cran-Orange Oatmeal Bars, 208
Cran-Raspberry Gelatin Salad, 66
Creamy Alfredo Seafood Lasagna, 84
Creamy Chile and Chicken Casserole, 56

Creamy Golden Mushroom Mashed
    Potatoes, 167
Creamy Spinach-Stuffed Portobellos, 170
Crunchy Veg•All® Tuna Casserole, 96
Crustless Salmon & Broccoli Quiche, 86

D
Delicious Ham & Cheese Puff Pie, 20
Double Chocolate Chip Snack Cake, 220
Double-Chocolate Pecan Brownies, 198
Double-Decker Confetti Brownies, 200
Double Peanut Butter Paisley Brownies,
    204

E
Easy Apple Butter Cake, 228
Easy Cheesy Bacon Bread, 122
Easy Microwave Brownies, 200
Egg Dishes
    Aunt Marilyn's Cinnamon French Toast
        Casserole, 2
    Bacon and Maple Grits Puff, 18
    Breakfast Bake, 4
    Brunch Eggs Olé, 12
    Crustless Salmon & Broccoli Quiche, 86
    Delicious Ham & Cheese Puff Pie, 20
    Hash Brown Casserole, 8
    Italian Vegetable Strata, 34
    Spinach Sensation, 16
    Summer Sausage 'n' Egg Wedges, 14
    Surimi Seafood-Zucchini Frittata with
        Fresh Tomato Sauce, 88
Enchilada Slow-Roasted Baby Back Ribs,
    147
English Bath Buns, 134

F
Farmer-Style Sour Cream Bread, 128
Farmhouse Lemon Meringue Pie, 192
Fennel Braised with Tomato, 166
Fiesta Pasta Salad, 72
Flan, 185
French Toast Strata, 10
Fresh Lime and Black Bean Soup, 98
Fresh Salsa, 12
Frostings & Glazes
    Cocoa Glaze, 216
    Peanut Butter Frosting, 180
Fudgy Hazelnut Brownies, 196

G
Garlic and Chipotle Cheddar Mashed
    Potatoes, 168
German Upside Down Cake, 210
Give Me S'more Muffins, 254
Glazed Parsnips and Carrots, 164
Good Old American White Rolls, 126
Greek Date-Nut Swirls, 236
Green Bean Casserole, 162
Green Chile Chicken Soup with Tortilla
    Dumplings, 116
Grilled Corn & Chicken Soup, 110
Grilled Ratatouille, 168

H
Ham
    Delicious Ham & Cheese Puff Pie, 20
    Ham 'n' Apple Breakfast Casserole Slices, 4
    Ham Seasoned Peas, 166
Hash Brown Casserole, 8
Hazelnuts: Fudgy Hazelnut Brownies, 196
Heartland Chicken Casserole, 46
Hearty Chicken Chili, 102
Hearty Vegetable Stew, 112
Hershey's Brownies with Peanut Butter
    Frosting, 180
Holiday Pumpkin Muffins, 252
Honey-Orange Spicecake, 222
Honey Pumpkin Pie, 260
Honey Whole-Grain Bread, 124

I
Italian Hillside Garden Soup, 108
Italian Mushroom Soup, 104
Italian Sausage Soup, 114
Italian Vegetable Strata, 34
It's a Keeper Casserole, 40

J
Jerk Pork and Sweet Potato Stew, 106

L
Lasagna
    Cousin Arlene's Spaghetti Lasagna, 50
    Creamy Alfredo Seafood Lasagna, 84
    Lasagna Supreme, 60
Layered Pasta Casserole, 54
Lemon Shrimp, 82

Loaded, Baked Potato Salad, 70
Louisiana Gumbo, 100

M

Mandarin Orange Tea Cake, 219
Marshmallows
    Chocolate Crispy Treat Cake, 226
    Give Me S'more Muffins, 254
Meat Loaves
    Cheese-Stuffed Meat Loaf, 148
    Old-Fashioned Meat Loaf, 138
Mediterranean-Style Tuna Noodle
    Casserole, 90
Mexican Tossed Layer Casserole, 44
Muffins, 246–259
Mushroom
    Asian Beef Stew, 112
    Baked Bow-Tie Pasta in Mushroom Cream
      Sauce, 30
    Creamy Chile and Chicken Casserole, 56
    Creamy Golden Mushroom Mashed
      Potatoes, 167
    Creamy Spinach-Stuffed Portobellos, 170
    Heartland Chicken Casserole, 46
    Italian Mushroom Soup, 104
    Lasagna Supreme, 60
    Lemon Shrimp, 82
    Mediterranean-Style Tuna Noodle
      Casserole, 90
    Pizza Soup, 100
    Southwestern Corn and Pasta Casserole, 38
    Steak Diane with Cremini Mushrooms, 152
    Turkey and Mushroom Wild Rice
      Casserole, 48
    Veggie-Stuffed Portobello Mushrooms, 22
    Wild Rice, Mushroom and Cranberry
      Dressing, 28

N

New York-Style Sour Cream-Topped
    Cheesecake, 182
Nine-Layer Salad, 68
Nuts *(see individual listings)*
    Banana Peanut Butter Chip Muffins, 258
    Chocolate Chunk Coffee Cake, 14
    Hershey's Brownies with Peanut Butter
      Frosting, 180
    Nutty Toffee Coffee Cake, 18
    Peanut Butter & Banana Cookies, 244

Nutty Oatmeal Raisin Chews, 242
Nutty Oven-Fried Chicken Drumsticks, 146
Nutty Toffee Coffee Cake, 18

O

Oat-Apricot Snack Cake, 218
Oatmeal Scotchies, 240
Oats
    Cherry-Almond Streusel Cake, 212
    Chunky Oatmeal Raisin Cookies, 234
    Cobbled Fruit Bars, 196
    Nutty Oatmeal Raisin Chews, 242
    Oat-Apricot Snack Cake, 218
    Oatmeal Scotchies, 240
    Old-Fashioned Meat Loaf, 138
    Rustic Plum Tart, 264
    Three-Grain Bread, 118
Old-Fashioned Cabbage Rolls, 51
Old-Fashioned Meat Loaf, 138
Old-Fashioned Pumpkin Pie, 276
Old-Fashioned Turkey Pot Pie, 42
Olives, Black
    Baked Red Snappers with Veg•All®, 82
    Sausage Pizza Pie Casserole, 42
Orange
    Asian Beef Stew, 112
    Cran-Orange Oatmeal Bars, 208
    Honey-Orange Spicecake, 222
    Mandarin Orange Tea Cake, 219
    Orange and Maple Glazed Roast Turkey,
      140
    Sesame Rice Salad, 70
Oven Barbecue Chicken, 142

P

Paella, 94
Parmesan Vegetable Bake, 31
Pasta & Noodles
    Baked Bow-Tie Pasta in Mushroom Cream
      Sauce, 30
    Baked Ravioli with Pumpkin Sauce, 34
    Cousin Arlene's Spaghetti Lasagna, 50
    Crab-Artichoke Casserole, 84
    Creamy Alfredo Seafood Lasagna, 84
    Crunchy Veg•All® Tuna Casserole, 96
    Fiesta Pasta Salad, 72
    Italian Hillside Garden Soup, 108
    Italian Sausage Soup, 114
    Lasagna Supreme, 60

Pasta & Noodles (*continued*)
Layered Pasta Casserole, 54
Lemon Shrimp, 82
Mediterranean-Style Tuna Noodle
Casserole, 90
Southwestern Corn and Pasta Casserole, 38
Southwest Pasta Salad, 68
Spicy Jac Mac & Cheese with Broccoli, 26
Tuna Tomato Casserole, 80
Veggie and Cheese Manicotti, 30

Peanut Butter
Banana Peanut Butter Chip Muffins, 258
Chewy Peanut Butter Brownies, 208
Double Peanut Butter Paisley Brownies, 204
Hershey's Brownies with Peanut Butter
Frosting, 180
Peanut Butter & Banana Cookies, 244
Peanut Butter Blossoms, 232
Peanut Butter Frosting, 180
Quick Peanut Butter Chocolate Chip
Cookies, 237

Pears: Rustic Cranberry-Pear Galette, 188

Peas
Asian Beef Stew, 112
Ham Seasoned Peas, 166
Mediterranean-Style Tuna Noodle
Casserole, 90
Nine-Layer Salad, 68
Paella, 94
Rainbow Casserole, 48
Sicilian Steak Pinwheels, 146

Pecans
Butterscotch Bundt Cake, 224
Chocolate Chunk Cookies, 230
Country Pecan Pie, 274
Cranberry Pecan Muffins, 250
Double-Chocolate Pecan Brownies, 198
German Upside Down Cake, 210
Nutty Oven-Fried Chicken Drumsticks, 146
Sweet 'n' Spicy Pecan Pie, 269
Turkey and Mushroom Wild Rice
Casserole, 48

Pesto Rice Salad, 74

Pies
Apple & Cherry Pie, 270
Classic Apple Pie, 274
Country Pecan Pie, 274
Farmhouse Lemon Meringue Pie, 192
Honey Pumpkin Pie, 260

Pies (*continued*)
Old-Fashioned Pumpkin Pie, 276
Spicy Pumpkin Pie, 272
Sweet 'n' Spicy Pecan Pie, 269

Pineapple
Carrot Pineapple Muffins, 253
Pineapple Carrot Raisin Muffins, 256
Pineapple Coffee Cake, 6
Spicy Citrus Pork with Pineapple Salsa, 156
Tapioca Fruit Salad, 78

Pistachio Walnut Bundt Cake, 224
Pizza Soup, 100
Plum Purée, 253

Plums
Plum Purée, 253
Rustic Plum Tart, 264

Porcupine Meatballs, 144

Pork (*see also* **Bacon**, **Ham** and **Sausage**)
Enchilada Slow-Roasted Baby Back Ribs,
147
Jerk Pork and Sweet Potato Stew, 106
Old-Fashioned Cabbage Rolls, 51
Pork and Corn Bread Stuffing Casserole, 58
Pork Chops with Cranberry-Jalapeño
Relish, 150
Spicy Citrus Pork with Pineapple Salsa, 156
Tuscan Roast Pork Tenderloin, 138

Potato, Cucumber and Dill Salad, 66

Potatoes (*see also* **Potatoes, Sweet**)
Baked Potato Soup, 107
Chunky Ranch Potatoes, 164
Creamy Golden Mushroom Mashed
Potatoes, 167
Garlic and Chipotle Cheddar Mashed
Potatoes, 168
Hash Brown Casserole, 8
Hearty Vegetable Stew, 112
Loaded, Baked Potato Salad, 70
Parmesan Vegetable Bake, 31
Potato, Cucumber and Dill Salad, 66
Rainbow Casserole, 48
Roasted Vegetable Salad with Capers and
Walnuts, 64
Shrimp Primavera Pot Pie, 90
Twice-Baked Potatoes with Sun-Dried
Tomatoes, 158

Potatoes, Sweet
Candied Sweet Potatoes, 172
Jerk Pork and Sweet Potato Stew, 106

Potatoes, Sweet (*continued*)
 Roasted Sweet Potato Salad, 71
 Thyme-Scented Roasted Sweet Potatoes
  and Onions, 162
Pounceole Salad, 76
Praline Pumpkin Tart, 268
Praline Topping, 269
Pumpkin
 Baked Ravioli with Pumpkin Sauce, 34
 Holiday Pumpkin Muffins, 252
 Honey Pumpkin Pie, 260
 Old-Fashioned Pumpkin Pie, 276
 Praline Pumpkin Tart, 268
 Pumpkin Chocolate Chip Muffins,
  248
 Pumpkin Custard, 186
 Pumpkin Harvest Bars, 201
 Spicy Pumpkin Pie, 272
Pumpkin Chocolate Chip Muffins, 248
Pumpkin Custard, 186
Pumpkin Harvest Bars, 201

Q
Quick Peanut Butter Chocolate Chip
  Cookies, 237
Quinoa-Stuffed Tomatoes, 26

R
Rainbow Casserole, 48
Raisins
 Chunky Oatmeal Raisin Cookies, 234
 Cobbled Fruit Bars, 196
 Holiday Pumpkin Muffins, 252
 Nutty Oatmeal Raisin Chews, 242
 Pineapple Carrot Raisin Muffins, 256
 Pumpkin Harvest Bars, 201
Raspberry Streusel Muffins, 246
Red, White and Blue Muffins, 250
Rice
 Baked Red Snappers with Veg•All®,
  82
 Louisiana Gumbo, 100
 Mexican Tossed Layer Casserole, 44
 Paella, 94
 Pesto Rice Salad, 74
 Porcupine Meatballs, 144
 Rio Bravo Rice-Stuffed Poblanos, 36
 Sesame Rice Salad, 70
 Shrimp Creole, 96

Rice (*continued*)
 Turkey and Mushroom Wild Rice
  Casserole, 48
 Wild Rice, Mushroom and Cranberry
  Dressing, 28
Rio Bravo Rice-Stuffed Poblanos, 36
Roasted Garlic Breadsticks, 130
Roasted Sweet Potato Salad, 71
Roasted Vegetable Salad with Capers and
  Walnuts, 64
Roman Meal® Cream of Rye Bread, 128
Rustic Cranberry-Pear Galette, 188
Rustic Plum Tart, 264

S
Sage Buns, 120
Salads, 62–79
Salmon: Crustless Salmon & Broccoli
  Quiche, 86
Salsa-Buttered Corn on the Cob, 160
Sausage
 Biscuit and Sausage Bake, 8
 Breakfast Bake, 4
 Chorizo Chili, 108
 Italian Sausage Soup, 114
 Lasagna Supreme, 60
 Layered Pasta Casserole, 54
 Paella, 94
 Sausage Pizza Pie Casserole, 42
 Sicilian Steak Pinwheels, 146
 Summer Sausage 'n' Egg Wedges, 14
Savory Garlic Steak with Charred Tomato
  Salsa, 142
Sesame Rice Salad, 70
Shrimp
 Lemon Shrimp, 82
 Louisiana Gumbo, 100
 Paella, 94
 Shrimp Creole, 96
 Shrimp Primavera Pot Pie, 90
Sicilian Steak Pinwheels, 146
Slow Cooker Recipes
 Asian Beef Stew, 112
 Chocolate Croissant Pudding, 176
 Chorizo Chili, 108
 Chunky Ranch Potatoes, 164
 Fresh Lime and Black Bean Soup, 98
 Hearty Chicken Chili, 102
 Honey Whole-Grain Bread, 124

Slow Cooker Recipes (*continued*)
Italian Hillside Garden Soup, 108
Italian Sausage Soup, 114
Jerk Pork and Sweet Potato Stew, 106
Pizza Soup, 100
Pumpkin Custard, 186
Sicilian Steak Pinwheels, 146
Spicy Citrus Pork with Pineapple Salsa, 156
Snapper: Baked Red Snappers with
Veg•All®, 82
Sonoma Dried Tomato and Vegetable
Biscuits, 122
Soups
Baked Potato Soup, 107
Fresh Lime and Black Bean Soup, 98
Green Chile Chicken Soup with Tortilla
Dumplings, 116
Grilled Corn & Chicken Soup, 110
Italian Hillside Garden Soup, 108
Italian Mushroom Soup, 104
Italian Sausage Soup, 114
Pizza Soup, 100
Spicy Squash & Chicken Soup, 106
Southern Buttermilk Fried Chicken, 136
Southwestern Chicken and Black Bean
Skillet, 154
Southwestern Corn and Pasta Casserole, 38
Southwestern Enchiladas, 44
Southwest Pasta Salad, 68
Spanish Stewed Tomatoes, 167
Spicy Cheese Bread, 132
Spicy Chicken Casserole with Corn Bread, 52
Spicy Citrus Pork with Pineapple Salsa, 156
Spicy Jac Mac & Cheese with Broccoli, 26
Spicy Pumpkin Pie, 272
Spicy Squash & Chicken Soup, 106
Spinach
Creamy Spinach-Stuffed Portobellos, 170
Delicious Ham & Cheese Puff Pie, 20
Italian Sausage Soup, 114
Layered Pasta Casserole, 54
Nine-Layer Salad, 68
Spinach Artichoke Gratin, 160
Spinach Sensation, 16
Squash (*see also* **Zucchini**)
Creamy Chile and Chicken Casserole, 56
Grilled Ratatouille, 168
Nine-Layer Salad, 68
Spicy Squash & Chicken Soup, 106

Steak Diane with Cremini Mushrooms, 152
Stew
Asian Beef Stew, 112
Hearty Vegetable Stew, 112
Jerk Pork and Sweet Potato Stew, 106
Summer Sausage 'n' Egg Wedges, 14
Surimi Seafood-Zucchini Frittata with Fresh
Tomato Sauce, 88
Sweet and Sour Brunch Cake, 216
Sweet 'n' Spicy Pecan Pie, 269
Sweetened Whipped Cream, 269

T

Tapioca Fruit Salad, 78
Tarts
Apple-Cranberry Tart, 266
Caramelized Onion Tart, 24
Cherry Frangipane Tart, 272
Chocolate Walnut Toffee Tart, 262
Praline Pumpkin Tart, 268
Rustic Cranberry-Pear Galette, 188
Rustic Plum Tart, 264
Three-Grain Bread, 118
Thyme-Cheese Bubble Loaf, 127
Thyme-Scented Roasted Sweet Potatoes and
Onions, 162
Toffee: Nutty Toffee Coffee Cake, 18
Tomatoes, Canned
Chorizo Chili, 108
Hearty Vegetable Stew, 112
Italian Hillside Garden Soup, 108
It's a Keeper Casserole, 40
Lasagna Supreme, 60
Louisiana Gumbo, 100
Paella, 94
Pizza Soup, 100
Rainbow Casserole, 48
Shrimp Creole, 96
Spanish Stewed Tomatoes, 167
Spicy Chicken Casserole with Corn Bread,
52
Spicy Squash & Chicken Soup, 106
Tomatoes, Fresh
Black Bean Flautas with Charred
Tomatillo Salsa, 32
Creamy Spinach-Stuffed Portobellos, 170
Crustless Salmon & Broccoli Quiche, 86
Fennel Braised with Tomato, 166
Fresh Salsa, 12

Tomatoes, Fresh *(continued)*
    Grilled Ratatouille, 168
    Lemon Shrimp, 82
    Mediterranean-Style Tuna Noodle
        Casserole, 90
    Nine-Layer Salad, 68
    Parmesan Vegetable Bake, 31
    Pesto Rice Salad, 74
    Quinoa-Stuffed Tomatoes, 26
    Sausage Pizza Pie Casserole, 42
    Savory Garlic Steak with Charred Tomato
        Salsa, 142
    Tuna Tomato Casserole, 80
Topsy-Turvy Banana Crunch Cake, 224
Tortilla Beef Casserole, 52
Tuna
    Crunchy Veg•All® Tuna Casserole, 96
    Mediterranean-Style Tuna Noodle
        Casserole, 90
    Tuna Tomato Casserole, 80
Turkey
    Louisiana Gumbo, 100
    Old-Fashioned Turkey Pot Pie, 42
    Orange and Maple Glazed Roast Turkey,
        140
    Pizza Soup, 100
    Turkey and Mushroom Wild Rice
        Casserole, 48
    Turkey Wienerschnitzel, 150
Tuscan Roast Pork Tenderloin, 138
Twice-Baked Potatoes with Sun-Dried
    Tomatoes, 158

V

Vanilla Whipped Cream (Creme Chantilly),
    276
Veggie and Cheese Manicotti, 30
Veggie-Stuffed Portobello Mushrooms, 22
Very Verde Green Bean Salad, 62

W

Walnuts
    Carrot Cake with Black Walnut Frosting,
        176
    Cherry Crisp, 178
    Chocolate Walnut Toffee Tart, 262
    Chunky Oatmeal Raisin Cookies, 234
    Cranberry Coffee Cake, 13
    Cran-Raspberry Gelatin Salad, 66

Walnuts *(continued)*
    Greek Date-Nut Swirls, 236
    Nutty Oatmeal Raisin Chews, 242
    Pineapple Coffee Cake, 6
    Pistachio Walnut Bundt Cake, 224
    Pumpkin Chocolate Chip Muffins, 248
    Roasted Vegetable Salad with Capers and
        Walnuts, 64
White Chocolate
    Double Chocolate Chip Snack Cake, 220
    Fudgy Hazelnut Brownies, 196
    Red, White and Blue Muffins, 250
Wild Rice, Mushroom and Cranberry
    Dressing, 28

Z

Zucchini
    Grilled Ratatouille, 168
    Italian Hillside Garden Soup, 108
    Italian Vegetable Strata, 34
    Parmesan Vegetable Bake, 31
    Surimi Seafood-Zucchini Frittata with
        Fresh Tomato Sauce, 88
    Veggie-Stuffed Portobello Mushrooms, 22

METRIC CONVERSION CHART

VOLUME MEASUREMENTS (dry)

1/8 teaspoon = 0.5 mL
1/4 teaspoon = 1 mL
1/2 teaspoon = 2 mL
3/4 teaspoon = 4 mL
1 teaspoon = 5 mL
1 tablespoon = 15 mL
2 tablespoons = 30 mL
1/4 cup = 60 mL
1/3 cup = 75 mL
1/2 cup = 125 mL
2/3 cup = 150 mL
3/4 cup = 175 mL
1 cup = 250 mL
2 cups = 1 pint = 500 mL
3 cups = 750 mL
4 cups = 1 quart = 1 L

VOLUME MEASUREMENTS (fluid)

1 fluid ounce (2 tablespoons) = 30 mL
4 fluid ounces (1/2 cup) = 125 mL
8 fluid ounces (1 cup) = 250 mL
12 fluid ounces (1 1/2 cups) = 375 mL
16 fluid ounces (2 cups) = 500 mL

WEIGHTS (mass)

1/2 ounce = 15 g
1 ounce = 30 g
3 ounces = 90 g
4 ounces = 120 g
8 ounces = 225 g
10 ounces = 285 g
12 ounces = 360 g
16 ounces = 1 pound = 450 g

DIMENSIONS

1/16 inch = 2 mm
1/8 inch = 3 mm
1/4 inch = 6 mm
1/2 inch = 1.5 cm
3/4 inch = 2 cm
1 inch = 2.5 cm

OVEN TEMPERATURES

250°F = 120°C
275°F = 140°C
300°F = 150°C
325°F = 160°C
350°F = 180°C
375°F = 190°C
400°F = 200°C
425°F = 220°C
450°F = 230°C

BAKING PAN SIZES

Utensil	Size in Inches/Quarts	Metric Volume	Size in Centimeters
Baking or Cake Pan (square or rectangular)	8×8×2	2 L	20×20×5
	9×9×2	2.5 L	23×23×5
	12×8×2	3 L	30×20×5
	13×9×2	3.5 L	33×23×5
Loaf Pan	8×4×3	1.5 L	20×10×7
	9×5×3	2 L	23×13×7
Round Layer Cake Pan	8×1½	1.2 L	20×4
	9×1½	1.5 L	23×4
Pie Plate	8×1¼	750 mL	20×3
	9×1¼	1 L	23×3
Baking Dish or Casserole	1 quart	1 L	—
	1½ quart	1.5 L	—
	2 quart	2 L	—